P9-BIY-265

Ontology — The Hermeneutics of Facticity

Studies in Continental Thought

GENERAL EDITOR

JOHN SALLIS

CONSULTING EDITORS

Robert Bernasconi
Rudolf Bernet
John D. Caputo
David Carr
Edward S. Casey
Hubert L. Dreyfus
Don Ihde
David Farrell Krell
Lenore Langsdorf
Alphonso Lingis

William L. McBride
J. N. Mohanty
Mary Rawlinson
Tom Rockmore
Calvin O. Schrag
† Reiner Schürmann
Charles E. Scott
Thomas Sheehan
Robert Sokolowski
Bruce W. Wilshire

David Wood

Martin Heidegger

Ontology — The Hermeneutics of Facticity

Translated by
John van Buren

Indiana University Press
Bloomington & Indianapolis

This book is a publication of

Indiana University Press
601 North Morton Street
Bloomington, Indiana 47404-3797 USA

www.indiana.edu/~iupress

Telephone orders 800-842-6796
Fax orders 812-855-7931
Orders by e-mail iuporder@indiana.edu

Published in German as Martin Heidegger, *Gesamtausgabe,* volume 63:
Ontologie (Hermeneutik der Faktizität), edited by Käte Bröcker-Oltmanns.

First paperback edition printed in 2008
© 1988 by Vittorio Klostermann, Frankfurt am Main
© 1999 by Indiana University Press
All rights reserved

No part of this book may be reproduced or utilized in any form or by
any means, electronic or mechanical, including photocopying and
recording, or by any information storage and retrieval system, without
permission in writing from the publisher. The Association of American
University Presses' Resolution on Permissions constitutes the only
exception to this prohibition.

The paper used in this publication meets the minimum requirements
of American National Standard for Information Sciences—
Permanence of Paper for Printed
Library Materials, ANSI Z39.48-1984.

Manufactured in the United States of America

Library of Congress Cataloging-in-Publication Data

Heidegger, Martin, 1889-1976.
[Ontologie. English]
Ontology : the hermeneutics of facticity / Martin Heidegger ;
translated by John van Buren.
p.   cm. — (Studies in Continental thought)
Includes bibliographical references.
ISBN 0-253-33507-8 (alk. paper)
1. Ontology. I. Title. II. Series.
B3279.H4806713 1999
111—dc21   98-54763
ISBN-13: 978-0-253-33507-4 (cl.)
ISBN-13: 978-0-253-22021-9 (pbk.)
4   5   6   7   13   12   11   10   09

Contents

Introduction

THE HERMENEUTICS OF FACTICITY

What is missing in the dialectic of today: looking in the direction of the actual object of philosophy. — It is this looking which develops unity. — Dialectic considers itself superior to phenomenology insofar as it sees itself as the higher stage of mediated knowledge which penetrates the irrational. — On the contrary: the most decisive factor is a fundamental looking in the direction of the subject matter. — Hegel's dialectic lives from the table of others. — Hegelese, sophistry. Cf. Brentano on it. — The danger in phenomenology: uncritical trust in evidence.

Our theme: the being-there of Dasein in the awhileness of temporal particularity. — "Object." — Dasein expresses itself in the public realm of educated consciousness. Talk. — What characteristic of the being of Dasein shows up in the above modes of its interpretation and its having-itself?

Chapter Four

Analysis of Each Interpretation
Regarding Its Mode of Being-Related to Its Object

"As what" is Dasein seen in each?

The past as an expression of something. — Fore-sight with respect to style. — This is the basis of preservation of the past being able to hold onto expressive networks of reference in a unified manner. — Foresight already operative in the fundamental work of historical research, i.e., in the critical choice of sources. — Uniform "whiling" or "tarrying" among all cultures. Universal classification which objectively compares forms. Never halting, making a sojourn, and holding out there. — The availability of the past. — Seven phenomenal characteristics of historical consciousness. — The character of its actualization: curiosity which is led and pulled along. — Spengler: history must be objective. — Just as it has a past, the Dasein which is interpreted in this manner also has its present and future. — Spengler's influence on special fields of history. — Imitation of history of art.

The question: how and as what does philosophy have its object in view? — An answer is lacking in today's philosophies. — What needs to be seen in the basic tendency of the systems themselves is that philosophy is universal classifying. — Its point of departure: the temporal, the concrete, understood in terms of essential generalities. — Either classifying and filing away into an extant framework, or the system first develops itself in the classifying and filing away. — Three modes of philosophical comporting. — Developing the totality of the classificatory order consists in running through the context of relations in which each is also the other. — The as-well-as is the fundamental structure of the absolute context of the classificatory order. — The appropriate comportment: universal movement, absolute curiosity which is everywhere and nowhere and leads itself along. — In the public realm, philosophy sees itself (1) as objective in opposition to relativism, (2) as universal agreement in opposition to skepticism, (3) as dynamic and true to life, and (4) as simultaneously universal and concrete in opposition to overly detailed specialization.

In both modes of interpretation, Dasein seeks to have itself objectively there for itself, to make itself objectively certain and secure about itself. — Curiosity: a movement of Dasein. — Dasein is this movement and at the same time has itself in it. — The characteristics of being-interpreted are categories of Dasein, existentials.

PART TWO
THE PHENOMENOLOGICAL PATH OF
THE HERMENEUTICS OF FACTICITY

Chapter One

"Phenomenon": what shows itself, a distinctive mode of being-an-object. — In the natural sciences it meant an object of experience. — The human sciences and philosophy oriented themselves to the natural sciences, concentrating on theory of science and psychology purportedly in the spirit of Kant. — On the contrary, the genuine way to imitate the natural sciences in Brentano: theories are to be drawn from the things themselves (psychical phenomena). — Husserl's *Logical Investigations:* phenomenology is descriptive psychology. The objects of logic are found in conscious experiences (consciousness of something = intentionality). — "Phenomenon" concerns the mode of access. "Phenomenology" is a mode of research. — A mistake: taking mathematics as the model. — The concept of phenomenon (the object as it shows itself) was then narrowed down to mean consciousness as an object. — External influences (epistemology, Dilthey, transcendental idealism, realism, etc.) and outwardly general wishy-washiness.

Phenomenology endeavors to take its objects just as they show themselves, i.e., for a definite manner of looking toward them and seeing them. — This arises out of and on the basis of an already-being-familiar with them, out of tradition. — But it can be a covering up. Thus historical critique as a fundamental task of philosophy. — The absence of history in "phenomenology," its plain and simple "evidence." — Regress to the Greeks. — Covering up belongs to the being of the object of philosophy, thus necessitating a constant preparation of the path to be traveled. — The radical task of hermeneutics: to make this object a phenomenon.

break forth. — Curiosity as a how of care. — Its masquerades. — Care: a fundamental phenomenon of the being-there of Dasein.

Appendix: Inserts and Supplements 81

Contents

Ontology—The Hermeneutics of Facticity

Lecture Course from the Summer Semester of 1923

INTRODUCTION

§1. The title "Ontology"[1]*

As comments on the first indication of the theme of facticity. Initial description: ontology.[2]

"Ontology" means doctrine of being. If we hear in this term only the indefinite and vague directive that, in the following, being should in some thematic way come to be investigated and come to language,[3] then the word has performed its possible service as the title of the course. However, if ontology is regarded as designating a discipline, one belonging, for instance, within the field of inquiry of Neo-Scholasticism or within that of phenomenological Scholasticism and the directions of academic philosophy influenced by it, then the word "ontology" is not as a course title fitting for what our theme and manner of treating it will be in the following.

If on top of that one takes "ontology" to be a rallying motto for the now popular attacks on Kant and, more precisely, on the spirit of Luther and, in principle, on all open questioning not frightened in advance by possible consequences—in short, ontology as the alluring call to a slave revolt against philosophy as such—then the title of this course is completely misleading.

The terms "ontology" and "ontological" will be used only in the above-mentioned empty sense of nonbinding indications. They refer to a questioning and defining which is directed to being as such. Which sort of being [*Sein*][4] is to be questioned after and defined and how this is to be done remain utterly indefinite.

In preserving a memory of the Greek word ὄν [being], "ontology" at the same time means that epigonic treatment of traditional questions about being which proliferates on the soil of classical Greek philosophy. Though traditional ontology claims to deal with general definitions of being, it actually has a definite region of being before its eyes.

In its modern usage, the word "ontology" means as much as "theory of objects" and indeed one which is in the first place formal. In this respect, it coincides with ancient ontology ("metaphysics").

However, modern ontology is not an isolated discipline, but rather is connected in a peculiar manner with what is understood by phenomenology in a narrow sense. *It was in phenomenology that a fitting concept of research first emerged.* Ontology of nature, ontology of culture, material

---

* Bracketed notes will be found in the Endnotes on the Translation. Footnotes designated by symbols are provided by the translator.

ontologies—they form the disciplines in which the content of the objects in these regions is drawn out as subject matter and displayed in its categorial character. What is thus made available then serves as a guide for problems of *constitution,* the structural and genetic contexts of *consciousness of* objects of this or that kind.

Conversely, it is only through phenomenology that the ontology corresponding to it is established on a secure basis and held on an orderly course in its treatment of problems. When we look at consciousness of . . . , the *of-which,* i.e., the character of a being as such insofar as it is an object, also becomes visible, and it is only in this manner that it becomes visible. The characteristics of objects in the respective regions of being are what is at issue in the ontologies. This is what they come to. Precisely not being as such, i.e., be-ing which is free of objects.[5] Phenomenology in the narrow sense as a phenomenology of constitution. Phenomenology in the wide sense as something which includes ontology.

In such ontology the question—from which field of being should the decisive meaning of being which is to guide the treatment of all problems in ontology be drawn?—is not at all posed. This question is unknown to it, and because of that its own provenance, the genesis of its meaning, remains closed off to it.

The fundamental *inadequacy of ontology* in the tradition and today is twofold:

1. From the very start, its theme is being-an-*object,* i.e., the objectivity of definite objects, and the object as it is given for an indifferent theoretical mean-ing,[6] or a material being-an-object for the particular sciences of nature and culture concerned with it, and by means of the regions of objects—should the need arise—the world, but not as it is from out of its being-there for Dasein[7] and the possibilities of this being-there, or also affixing other nontheoretical characteristics to it. (Note: double sense of "nature" as world and as region of objects—"nature" as world can be formalized only from out of Dasein, historicity, thus not the "basis" of its temporality—same goes for "body.")

2. What results from this: it blocks access to that being [*Seienden*] which is decisive within philosophical problems: namely, *Dasein,* from out of which and for the sake of which, philosophy "is."

Insofar as the title "Ontology" is taken in an empty nonbinding sense, so that it means any questioning and investigating which is directed to being as such, it will indeed come into use in the following. Thus the term "ontological" refers to the posing of questions, explications, concepts, and categories which have arisen from looking at beings as be-ing [*Seiendes als Sein*] or, alternately, have failed to do this.

(Ancient metaphysics is taken up again as "ontology"—superstition and dogmatism without the slightest possibility of, or even mere tendency to, the kind of research which poses questions.)

(In "time" it will in fact be pointed out that fundamental problems are also found in ontology!)

Thus the course title which has arisen from the basic theme of what follows and the manner of its treatment is rather: *The Hermeneutics of Facticity.*

THE HERMENEUTICS OF FACTICITY

Foreword[1]

Putting forth *questions*—questions are not happenstance thoughts, nor are questions the common "problems" of today which "one"[8] picks up from hearsay and book learning and decks out with a gesture of profundity. Questions grow out of a confrontation with "subject matter." And subject matter is *there* only where eyes are.

It is in this manner that a number of questions will have to be "posed" in this course, and all the more so considering that questioning has today fallen out of fashion in the great industry of "problems." Here one is in fact secretly at work abolishing questioning altogether and is intent on cultivating the modesty of blind faith. One declares the *sacrum* [sacred] to be an essential law and is thereby taken seriously by one's age, which in its frailty and impotence has need for such a thing. One stands up for nothing more than the trouble-free running of the "industry"! Having become ripe for the organization of mendacity. Philosophy interprets its corruption as the "resurrection of metaphysics."

Companions in my searching were the young Luther and the paragon Aristotle, whom Luther hated. Impulses were given by Kierkegaard, and Husserl opened my eyes. This for those who "understand" something only when they reckon it up in terms of historical influences, the pseudo-understanding of an industrious curiosity, i.e., diversion from what is solely at issue in this course and what it all comes to. One should make their "tendency of understanding" as easy as possible for them so that they will perish of themselves. Nothing is to be expected of them. They care only about the pseudo.

---

1. Heidegger's title. The "Foreword" was not delivered in the course.

PART ONE

PATHS OF INTERPRETING THE BEING-THERE OF DASEIN IN THE AWHILENESS OF TEMPORAL PARTICULARITY

"*Facticity*" is the designation we will use for the character of the being of "our" "own" *Dasein*. More precisely, this expression means: *in each case* "this" Dasein in its being-there *for a while at the particular time* (the phenomenon of the "awhileness" of temporal particularity, cf. "whiling," tarrying for a while, not running away, being-*there*-at-home-in . . . , being-*there*-involved-in . . . , the being-there of Dasein) insofar as it is, in the character of its being, "*there*" *in the manner of be-ing*.[9] Being-there *in the manner of be-ing* means: not, and never, to be there primarily as an *object* of intuition and definition on the basis of intuition, as an *object* of which we merely take cognizance and have knowledge. Rather, Dasein is *there* for itself in the "how" of its ownmost being. The how of its being opens up and circumscribes[10] the respective "there" which is possible for a while at the particular time. Being—transitive: to be factical life! Being is itself never the possible object of a having, since what is at issue in it, what it comes to, is itself: *being*.

As that which is in each case our own, "Dasein" does not mean an isolating relativization into individuals who are seen only from the outside and thus the individual (*solus ipse* [myself alone]). "Our own" is rather a how of being, an indication which points to a possible path of being-wakeful. Not a regional demarcation in the sense of an isolating contrast.

Accordingly, "*factical*" means something which is of itself articulated with respect to, on the basis of, and with a view to such a *factical* character of being and "is" in this manner. If we take "life" to be a mode of "being," then "factical life" means: our own Dasein which is "there" for us in one expression or another of the character of its being, and this expression, too, is in the manner of being.

Chapter One

Hermeneutics

§2. The traditional concept of hermeneutics

The expression *"hermeneutics"* is used here to indicate the unified manner of the engaging, approaching, accessing, interrogating, and explicating of facticity.

The word ἑρμηνευτική [hermeneutics] (ἐπιστήμη [science], τέχνη [art]) is formed from ἑρμηνεύειν [interpreting], ἑρμηνεία [interpretation], ἑρμηνεύς [interpreter]. Its etymology is obscure.[1]

It is related to the name of the god Ἑρμῆς [Hermes], the messenger of the gods.

A few references will allow us to narrow down the original meaning of this word and understand as well the way its meaning has changed.

Plato: οἱ δὲ ποιηταὶ οὐδὲν ἀλλ᾽ ἢ ἑρμηνῆς εἰσιν τῶν θεῶν ("the poets are but the *heralds* of the gods").[2] Thus the following applies to the rhapsodes who for their part recite the poets: Οὐκοῦν ἑρμηνέων ἑρμηνῆς γίγνεσθε; "Will you not thus turn out to be heralds of heralds?"[3] A ἑρμηνεύς [interpreter] is one who communicates, announces and makes known,[11] to someone what another "means," or someone who in turn conveys, reactivates, this communication, this announcement and making known. Cf. *Sophist* 248a5, 246e3: ἀφερμήνευε, "shall report about"*: making known what the others mean.

Theaetetus 209a5: Λόγος [discourse] = ἡ τῆς σῆς διαφορότητος ἑρμηνεία [the expression of differences]. The making known is a making explicit of differences in addition to and in relation to what is κοινόν [common].† (cf. *Theaetetus* 163c: what we see of the words and what interpreters of them

1. Cf. É. Boisacq, *Dictionnaire étymologique* (Heidelberg and Paris, 1916), p. 282f.
2. *Ion*, ed. Burnet (Oxford, 1904), 534e. [Cf. Edith Hamilton and Huntington Cairns (eds.), *The Collected Dialogues of Plato* (Princeton: Princeton University Press, 1961), p. 220: ". . . these lovely poems are not of man or human workmanship, but are divine and from the gods, and the poets are nothing but interpreters of the gods. . . ."]
3. Ibid., 535a. [Cf. *The Collected Dialogues of Plato*, p. 221 (modified): "Well, and you rhapsodes, again, interpret the utterances of the poets? . . . Accordingly, you are interpreters of interpreters?"]
* Cf. *The Collected Dialogues of Plato*, p. 992: "Let us turn, then, to the opposite party, the friends of the forms. Once more you shall act as their spokesman [ἀφερμήνευε]."
† Cf. *The Collected Dialogues of Plato*, p. 917 (modified): "And 'account' [λόγος] means putting into words [ἑρμηνεία] your differentness. . . . at the time I had only a notion of you, my mind did not grasp any of the points in which you differ from others. . . . I must have had before my mind one of those common [κοινῶν] things which belong to another person as much as to you."

communicate.)‡ — not theoretical comprehension but "will," wish, and the like, being, existence, i.e., hermeneutics is the announcement and making known of the being of a being in its being in relation to . . . (me).

Aristotle: τῇ γλώττῃ (καταχρῆται ἡ φύσις) ἐπί τε τὴν γεῦσιν καὶ τὴν διάλεκτον, ὧν ἡ μὲν γεῦσις ἀναγκαῖον (διὸ καὶ πλείοσιν ὑπάρχει), ἡ δ' ἑρμηνεία ἕνεκα τοῦ εὖ. "Living beings use their tongue for tasting as well as for conversing as they go about their dealings[12]; of these, tasting is a necessary mode of their dealings (hence it is found in most of them), but addressing and discussing something with others (conversation about something) exists in order to safeguard the authentic being of living beings (as they live in their world and by means of it)."[4] Here ἑρμηνεία simply *stands for* διάλεκτος [conversation], i.e., discussing the world as we go about dealings with it. And such discussion is simply the factical mode of the actualizing of λόγος, and this (discourse about something) has as its concern δηλοῦν { . . . } τὸ συμφέρον καὶ τὸ βλαβερόν (i.e., discourse "*makes* beings openly manifest, *accessible* for our seeing and having of them in their expediency and inexpediency").[5]

See also ἑρμηνεύειν, Philostratus.[6] *Simplicii in Aristotelis Physicorum Commentaria.*[7] Pericles in Thucydides: καίτοι ἐμοὶ τοιούτῳ ἀνδρὶ ὀργίζεσθε ὃς οὐδενὸς οἴομαι ἥσσων εἶναι γνῶναί τε τὰ δέοντα καὶ ἑρμηνεῦσαι ταῦτα, φιλόπολίς τε καὶ χρημάτων κρείσσων. ["And yet I, with whom you are angry, am as competent as any man, I think, to

---

‡ Cf. *The Collected Dialogues of Plato,* p. 868: "The shape and color of the letters we both see and know; we hear and at the same time know the rising and falling accents of the voice. But we neither perceive by sight and hearing nor yet know what a schoolmaster or interpreter [ἑρμηνεὺς] could tell us about them."

4. *De anima* B 8, 420b18ff. [Cf. Richard McKeon (ed.), *The Basic Works of Aristotle* (New York: Random House, 1941), p. 572: ". . . the tongue is used for both tasting and articulating; in that case of the two functions tasting is necessary for the animal's existence (hence it is found more widely distributed), while articulate speech is a luxury subserving its possessor's well-being. . . ."]

5. *Politics* A 2, 1253a14f. [Cf. *The Basic Works of Aristotle,* p. 1129: ". . . the power of speech is intended to set forth the expedient and inexpedient. . . ."]

6. *De Vitis Sophistarum,* ed. C. L. Kayser (Leipzig, 1871), Vol. II, p. 11, l. 29, to be found also in H. Diels, *Die Fragmente der Vorsokratiker* (Berlin, 1912), Vol. II, p. 235, l. 19. [*The Lives of the Sophists,* trans. Wilmer Cave Wright (London: Heinemann, 1922), pp. 30–31 (modified): ". . . if we reflect on how many additions Aeschylus made to tragedy . . . , then we find that this is what Gorgias in his turn did for his fellow craftsmen. For he set an example to the sophists with . . . his daring and unusual manner of announcing (ἑρμηνεύειν) grand matters in a grand style. . . ."]

7. H. Diels (ed.), *Commentaria in Aristotelem Graeca,* Vol. 9 (Berlin, 1882), p. 329, l. 20. [Simplicius, *On Aristotle's Physics 2,* trans. Barrie Fleet (Ithaca: Cornell University Press, 1997), pp. 88–89 (modified): "Alexander criticizes as ungrammatical the textual reading 'why none of the thinkers of old . . . made no definitive statement about chance.' 'For (Aristotle) should,' Alexander says, 'have written "made any definite statement," because the negative is already there in the word "none".' . . . We should rather admire the passage for its clear and accurate manner of expression (ἑρμηνευμένον), which commands respect."]

know and announce the right measures, and as good a patriot and superior to the influence of money."]⁸

Aristotle: λέγω δέ, . . . , λέξιν εἶναι τὴν διὰ τῆς ὀνομασίας ἑρμηνείαν. [I mean that . . . the language is making something known through words."]⁹

Among the "writings" of Aristotle, one has been handed down with the title Περὶ ἑρμηνείας [On Interpretation]. It deals with λόγος in terms of its basic accomplishment of uncovering beings and making us familiar with them. The title of this text is very fitting in light of what was noted above. However, neither Aristotle nor his immediate successors in the Peripatos introduced the text under this title. It was handed down from Aristotle's literary estate to his students as an "unfinished draft" and "without a title." The title was already in use in the time of Andronicus of Rhodes. H. Meier, who has established the authenticity of the text on solid grounds, conjecturally puts the earliest appearance of the title in the first generation after Theophrastus and Eudemus.¹⁰

In the present context, what is solely important for us about ἑρμηνεία functioning as the title of Aristotle's particular investigation is what this tells us about the history of the meaning of this word. What discourse accomplishes is making something accessible as being there out in the open, as being available. As such, λόγος has, regarding what it accomplishes, the distinctive possibility of ἀληθεύειν [being-true] (making what was previously concealed, covered up, available as unconcealed, as there out in the open). Because Aristotle's text deals with all this, it is rightly called περὶ ἑρμηνείας.

This sense of ἑρμηνεύειν took on a general meaning among the Byzantines and corresponds to our term "to mean." A word or combination of words means something, "has a meaning." (A Platonism of meaning deriving from this.)

Philo describes Moses as a ἑρμηνεύς θεοῦ [interpreter of God], a messenger who announces and makes known the will of God.¹¹

Aristeas: τά τῶν Ἰουδαίων γράμματα "ἑρμηνείας προσδεῖται" (the

---

8. De bello Peloponnesiaco, ed. G. Boehme (Leipzig, 1878), Bk. II, 60 (5), p. 127. [History of the Peloponnesian War, Vol. I, trans. Charles Forster Smith (London: William Heinemann, 1921), p. 363 (modified).]

9. Poetics 6, 1450b13f. [The Poetics (London: Heinemann, 1965), p. 29 (modified).]

10. "Die Echtheit der Aristotelischen Hermeneutik," Archiv für Geschichte der Philosophie 13, NF. 6 (1900): 23-72.

11. De vita Mosis III, 23 (II, 188), in Opera IV, ed. L. Cohn (Berlin, 1902), p. 244. [Cf. Philo, Vol. 6, trans. F. H. Colson (London: Heinemann, 1929), p. 543 (modified): ". . . and I will now go on to show in conclusion that Moses was a prophet of the highest quality. Now I am fully aware that all things written in the sacred books are oracles delivered through Moses. . . . Of these divine utterances, some are spoken by God in his own person with his prophet as his interpreter."]

writings of the Jews "require translation," "interpretation").[12] Translation: making what was presented in a *foreign* language accessible in our own language and for the sake of it. In the Christian churches, ἑρμηνεία then came to mean as much as commentary (*enarratio*): ἑρμηνεία εἰς τὴν ὀκτάτευχον ["commentary on the Octateuch"]. Commenting, interpreting: pursuing what is authentically meant in a text and thereby making the matters which are meant accessible, facilitating access to them. ἑρμηνεία = ἐξήγησις [exegesis].

Augustine provides the first "hermeneutics" in grand style. *Homo timens Deum, voluntatem ejus in Scripturis sanctis diligenter inquirit. Et ne amet certamina, pietate mansuetus; praemunitus etiam scientia linguarum, ne in verbis locutionibusque ignotis haereat; praemunitus etiam cognitione quarumdam rerum necessariarum, ne vim naturamve earum quae propter similitudinem adhibentur, ignoret; adjuvante etiam codicum veritate, quam solers emendationis diligentia procuravit: veniat ita instructus ad ambigua Scripturarum discutienda atque solvenda.*

"Man should approach the interpretation of ambiguous passages in Scripture with the following provisions: in fear of God, with the sole care of seeking God's will in Scripture; thoroughly educated in piety lest he should take pleasure in falling into quarrels over words; equipped with knowledge of languages lest he should get hung up on unfamiliar words and locutions; supplied with knowledge of certain natural objects and events which are introduced for purposes of illustration, lest he should misjudge the strength of their evidence; supported by the truth which the texts contain. . . ."[13]

In the 17th century, we meet up with the title *Hermeneutica sacra* [*Sacred Hermeneutics*] for what is otherwise designated as *Clavis Scripturae sacrae*[14] [*A Key to Sacred Scripture*], *Isagoge ad sacras literas*[15] [*Introduction to Sacred Writings*], *Tractatus de interpretatione*[16] [*Treatise on Interpretation*], and *Philologia sacra*[17] [*Sacred Philology*].

---

12. *Ad Philocratem epistula,* ed. P. Wendland (Leipzig, 1890), p. 4, l. 3. [Cf. *Aristeas to Philocrates (Letter of Aristeas),* trans. Moses Hadas (New York: Harper & Brothers, 1951), p. 97 (modified): "Demetrius said, 'Translation is required. In the country of the Jews they use a peculiar script, just as the Egyptians employ their arrangement of letters, and they have their own language. They are supposed to use Syrian, but that is not the case, for theirs is another dialect.'"]

13. *De doctrina christiana,* in *Patrologia latina,* ed. Migne (subsequently cited as "Migne"), Vol. XXXIV (Paris, 1845), Liber III, cap. 1, 1, p. 65. [Cf. *On Christian Doctrine,* trans. D. W. Robertson (Indianapolis: Bobbs-Merrill, 1958), p. 78.]

14. M. Flacius Illyricus, *Clavis scripturae sanctae seu de sermone sacrarum literarum* (Basel, 1567).

15. S. Pagnino, *Isagogae ad sacras literas Liber unicus* (Cologne, 1540 and 1542).

16. W. Frantze, *Tractatus theologicus novus et perspicuus de interpretatione sacrarum scripturarum maxime legitima* (Wittenberg, 1619).

17. S. Glass, *Philologia sacra, qua totius V. et N. T. scripturae tum stylus et litteratura, tum sensus et genuinae interpretationis ratio expenditur* (Jena, 1623).

Hermeneutics is now no longer interpretation itself, but a doctrine about the conditions, the objects, the means, and the communication and practical application of interpretation. Cf. Johannes Jakob Rambach:

I. "De fundamentis hermeneuticae sacrae"[18] ["On the Principles of Sacred Hermeneutics"]. On the right plan of approach for the interpretation of texts, of the meaning of the texts.

II. "De mediis hermeneuticae sacrae domesticis"[19] ["On the Internal Means of Sacred Hermeneutics"]. Religious analogy as a principle of interpretation. Circumstances, affects. Arrangement, relations. Parallelism in Scripture.

III. "De mediis hermeneuticae sacrae externis et litterariis"[20] ["On the External and Literal Means of Sacred Hermeneutics"]. Grammatical, critical, rhetorical, logical, and scientific ones. Translation and commentary.

IV. "De sensus inventi legitima tractatione"[21] ["On the Proper Treatment of Discovered Meaning"]. On communication, supplying arguments, porismatic and practical application. (*Porismata* [inferences], πορίζειν: "to infer" in the sense of drawing conclusions.)[13]

With Schleiermacher, the idea of hermeneutics which had formerly been viewed in a comprehensive and living manner (cf. Augustine!) was then reduced to an "art {technique} of understanding"[22] another's discourse, and seen as a discipline connected with grammar and rhetoric, it was brought into relation with dialectic—this methodology is formal, as "general hermeneutics" (theory and technique of understanding any foreign discourse) it encompasses the special disciplines of theological and philological hermeneutics.

A. Boeckh took up this idea of hermeneutics in his *Encyclopedia and Methodology of Philological Disciplines.*[23]

Dilthey adopted Schleiermacher's concept of hermeneutics, defining it as "the formulation of rules of understanding" ("technique of inter-

---

18. *Institutiones hermeneuticae sacrae, variis observationibus copiosissimisque exemplis biblicis illustratae* (Jena, 1723), *Conspectus totius libri: Liber primus.*

19. Ibid., *Liber secundus.*

20. Ibid., *Liber tertius.*

21. Ibid., *Liber quartus.*

22. *Hermeneutik und Kritik m. bes. Beziehung auf das Neue Testament*, ed. F. Lücke, in *Sämmtliche Werke*, Part I, Vol. 7 (Berlin, 1838), p. 7. [*Hermeneutics: The Handwritten Manuscripts*, ed. Heinz Kimmerle, trans. James Duke and Jack Forstman (Missoula: Scholars Press, 1977), p. 96.]

23. *Encyklopädie und Methodologie der philologischen Wissenschaften* (Leipzig, 1877). [*On Interpretation and Criticism*, trans. John Paul Pritchard (Norman: University of Oklahoma Press, 1968).]

preting written records"),[24] but he supported it with an analysis of understanding as such and investigated the development of hermeneutics in the context of his research on the development of the human sciences.

But it is precisely here that a disastrous limitation in his position shows itself. The decisive epochs in the actual development of hermeneutics (Patristic period and Luther) remained hidden from him, since he always investigated hermeneutics as a theme only to the extent that it displayed a tendency to what he himself considered to be its essential dimension — a methodology for the hermeneutical human sciences. Still, the systematically conducted watering down of Dilthey's thought today (Spranger) has never once come close to measuring up to his position on the nature of hermeneutics, which is to start with already quite limited, showing little clarity regarding fundamental issues, and moving only to a small extent in their direction.

§3. Hermeneutics as the self-interpretation of facticity

In the title given to the following investigation, "hermeneutics" is *not* being used in its modern meaning, and in no sense does it have the meaning of such a broadly conceived doctrine *about* interpretation. In connection with its original meaning, this term means rather: a definite unity in the actualizing of ἑρμηνεύειν (of communicating), i.e., of the *interpreting of facticity* in which facticity is being encountered, seen, grasped, and expressed in concepts.

This word was chosen and is being used in its original meaning because, though basically inadequate, it nonetheless highlights in an indicative manner a few factors which are at work in the investigation of facticity. When looked at from the side of its "object," hermeneutics — as this object's presumed mode of access — clearly shows that this object has its being as something capable of interpretation and in need of interpretation and that to be in some state of having-been-interpreted belongs to its being. Hermeneutics has the task of making the Dasein which is in each case our own accessible to this Dasein itself with regard to the character of its being, communicating Dasein to itself in this regard, hunting down the alienation from itself with which it is smitten. In hermeneutics what is developed for Dasein is a possibility of its becoming and being for itself in the manner of an *understanding* of itself.

---

24. "Die Entstehung der Hermeneutik," in *Philosophische Abhandlungen, Chr. Sigwart zu seinem 70. Geburtstage gewidmet v. B. Erdmann u. a.* (Tübingen, Freiburg, and Leipzig, 1900), p. 190; 5th ed. in *Gesammelte Schriften*, Vol. V (Stuttgart and Göttingen, 1968), p. 320. ["The Development of Hermeneutics," in *Selected Writings*, trans. H. P. Rickman (Cambridge: Cambridge University Press, 1976), pp. 249-50 (modified).]

This understanding which arises in interpretation cannot at all be compared to what is elsewhere called understanding in the sense of a knowing comportment toward the life of another. It is not comportment toward . . . (intentionality) in any sense, but rather a *how of Dasein* itself. Terminologically, it may be defined in advance as the *wakefulness* of Dasein for itself.

Hermeneutics is not an artificially devised mode of analysis which is imposed on Dasein and pursued out of curiosity. What needs to be brought into relief from out facticity itself is *in what way* and *when* it calls for the kind of interpretation put forth. The relationship here between hermeneutics and facticity is not a relationship between the grasping of an object and the object grasped, in relation to which the former would simply have to measure itself. Rather, interpreting is itself a possible and distinctive how of the character of being of facticity. Interpreting is a being which belongs to the being of factical life itself.[14] If one were to describe facticity—improperly—as the "object" of hermeneutics (as plants are described as the objects of botany), then one would find this (hermeneutics) in its own object itself (as if analogously plants, what and how they are, came along with botany and from it).

This relationship with its "object" which, as we have just indicated, hermeneutics enjoys on the level of being makes the inception, execution, and appropriation of hermeneutics prior ontologically and factico-temporally to all accomplishments in the sciences. The chance that hermeneutics will go wrong belongs in principle to its ownmost being. The kind of evidence found in its explications is fundamentally labile. To hold up before it such an extreme ideal of evidence as "intuition of essences" would be a misunderstanding of what it can and should do.

The theme of this hermeneutical investigation is the Dasein which is in each case our own and indeed as hermeneutically interrogated with respect to and on the basis of[15] the character of its being and with a view to developing in it a radical wakefulness for itself. The being of factical life is distinctive in that it *is* in the how of the being of its *being-possible*. The *ownmost* possibility of be-ing itself which Dasein (facticity) is, and indeed without this possibility being "there" for it, may be designated as *existence*. It is with respect to this authentic be-ing itself that facticity is placed into our forehaving when initially engaging it and bringing it into play[16] in our hermeneutical questioning. It is from out of it, on the basis of it, and with a view to it that facticity will be interpretively explicated. The conceptual explicata which grow out of this interpretation are to be designated as *existentials*.

A *"concept"* is not a schema but rather a possibility of being, of how matters look in the moment [*des Augenblicks*], i.e., is constitutive of the moment—a meaning drawn out of something—points to a *forehaving*, i.e., transports us into a fundamental experience—points to a *foreconcep-*

tion, i.e., calls for a how of addressing and interrogating—i.e., transports us into the *being-there of our Dasein* in accord with its tendency to interpretation and its worry.[17] Fundamental concepts are not later additions to Dasein, but rather ex-press it in advance and propel it forward: grasping Dasein and stirring it by way of their pointing.[18]

The forehaving of interpretation—that it cannot be made present as the thematic object of a straightforward and exhaustive account is precisely a clear sign of the character of its being. As constitutive—and indeed in a decisive manner—of interpretation, which is itself *part and parcel* of the "being *there*" of Dasein [*das* da *sein*], it shares in the *character of Dasein's being: being-possible.* This being-possible is one which is circumscribed, modifying itself in a factical manner from out of the situation with respect to, on the basis of, and with a view *to* which hermeneutical questioning is operating in the particular case. The forehaving is therefore not something arbitrary and according to whim.

"Life can be interpreted only after it has been lived, just as Christ did not begin to explain the Scriptures and show how they taught of him until after he was resurrected" (Kierkegaard, journal, 4-15-1838).[1]

Fundamental questionableness in hermeneutics and of its being-with-a-view-to: The object: Dasein is Dasein only in it *itself.*[19] It *is,* though as the *being-on-the-way* of itself to *itself!* This kind of being which belongs to hermeneutics cannot be done away with or treated in an artificial and vicarious manner. It must be reckoned with in a decisive way. What is revealed in it is how the *anticipatory leap forward and running in advance* should be undertaken and can only be undertaken. The anticipatory leap forward: not positing an end, but reckoning with being-on-the-way, giving *it* free play, disclosing it, holding fast to *being-possible.*

To it corresponds a fundamental *questionableness* in forehaving. It is relucent in all characteristics of being—*ontic questionableness: caring,* unrest, anxiety, *temporality.*[20] It is in questionableness and in it alone that *the* position can be taken in which and for which there could be something like: "fixing" on an end. This only where what is fixed on, or what is not fixed on, *has being* as a how of Dasein! How is the problem of death related to this?

Only in hermeneutics can the position be developed in which we are in a position to question radically, without having to be guided by the traditional idea of man. (Having this as something questionable—how the problem of disposition is to be posed, or whether at all. Seen from the point of view of questionableness, does not *being-possible* become visible as something autonomously and concretely existential?[21])

---

1. *Die Tagebücher 1834-1855. Auswahl und Übertragung v. Th. Haecker* (Leipzig, no date), p. 92 (Munich, 4th ed., 1953, p. 99). [*Søren Kierkegaard's Journals and Papers,* Vol. 1, trans. Howard V. Hong (Bloomington: Indiana University Press, 1967), p. 449 (modified).]

Furthermore: interpretation begins in the "today,"[22] i.e., in the definite and average state of understanding from out of which and on the basis of which philosophy lives and *back* into which it *speaks*. The *"every-one"*[23] has to do with something definite and positive—it is not only a phenomenon of fallenness, but as such also a how of factical Dasein.

The scope of factical understanding cannot ever be calculated and worked out in advance. Likewise, the manner in which such understanding is developed cannot be subjected to the norms at work in the grasping and communication of mathematical theorems. This is at bottom inconsequential, since hermeneutics engages itself and brings itself into play in the situation and by starting from there understanding is possible for it.

There is no "generality" in hermeneutical understanding over and above what is formal. And if there were such a thing, any hermeneutics which rightly understood itself would see itself required to hold to the task of dis-tancing itself from it, calling attention to Dasein which is in each case factical, and thereby returning to it. The "formal" is never something autonomous, but rather only a disburdening and relief found in the world. What hermeneutics is really meant to achieve is not merely taking cognizance of something and having knowledge about it, but rather an existential knowing, i.e., a *being* [*ein* Sein]. It speaks *from out of* interpretation and for the sake of it.

The *initial hermeneutical engagement and bringing into play*—that with respect to, on the basis of, and with a view to which everything is like a card in a game staked—thus *the "as what"* in terms of which facticity is grasped in advance and stirred, the decisive character of its being initially put forth and brought into play, is not something which can be fabricated—nor is it, however, a readymade possession but rather arises and develops out of a fundamental experience, and here this means a philosophical wakefulness, in which Dasein is encountering[24] itself. The wakefulness is philosophical—this means: it lives and is at work in a primordial *self-interpretation* which philosophy has given of itself and which is such that philosophy constitutes a decisive possibility and mode of Dasein's self-encounter.

The basic content of this *self-communication* and *self-understanding* which philosophy has about itself must be capable of being brought into relief, and a preliminary indication of it needs to be given. What it says for this hermeneutics is: (1) Philosophy is a mode of knowing which is in factical life itself and in which factical Dasein is ruthlessly dragged back to itself and relentlessly thrown back upon itself. (2) As this mode of knowing, philosophy has no mission to take care of universal humanity and culture, to release coming generations once and for all from care about questioning, or to interfere with them simply through wrongheaded claims to validity. Philosophy is what it can be only as a philosophy of "its time." "Temporality." Dasein works in the how of its *being-now*.

But this could not be further from meaning that we are supposed to be as modern as possible, i.e., respond to the purported needs and imagined wants of the day being publicly voiced. Everything modern is recognizable in the fact that it artfully steals away from its own time and is capable of creating an "effect" only in this fashion. (Industry, propaganda, proselytizing, cliquish monopolies, intellectual racketeering.)

By contrast, as what Dasein happens to encounter itself, i.e., the character of its being, when its wakefulness has been led forth in such a manner cannot be calculated and worked out in advance and is not a matter for universal humanity or for a public, but rather is in each case the definite and decisive possibility of concrete facticity. The more we succeed in bringing facticity hermeneutically into our grasp and into concepts, the more transparent this possibility becomes. At "the same time," however, it is of itself something which uses itself up. As Dasein's historical *possibility* which is in each case definite and for a while at the particular time,[25] existence has as such already been ruined when one works with the idea that it can be made present in advance for philosophical curiosity to get a picture of it. Existence is never an "object," but rather being—it is *there* only insofar as in each case a living "is" it.

Insofar as the initial engagement and bringing into play is there for us only *in such a manner*, it is not an object for universal rationalization and public discussion. These are simply the prized means with which one in good time steers away from the possibility of *hitting upon* factical Dasein and *striking out* into it. Demands often and loudly proclaimed today: (1) everyone should avoid dwelling too much on presuppositions and look rather at the things themselves (a philosophy of things), (2) presuppositions must be put before the public in generally understandable terms, i.e., in the least dangerous and most plausible fashion—both demands surround themselves with the pretense of a purely objective, absolute philosophy. But they are only the masked cries of *anxiety* in the face of philosophy.

To ask where it is, then, that this hermeneutics belongs within the framework of the tasks of philosophy "itself" is a very peripheral and at bottom inconsequential question, if not one which has been posed in a fundamentally mistaken manner. The incidental strangeness of the course title should not tempt one to abandon oneself to such empty reflections.

Hermeneutics will itself remain unimportant so long as the wakefulness for facticity which it is supposed to temporalize and unfold[26] is not "there"—all talking *about it* is a fundamental misunderstanding of it. As far as I am concerned, if this personal comment is permitted, I think that hermeneutics is not philosophy at all, but in fact something preliminary which runs in advance of it and has its own reason for being: what is at issue in it, what it all comes to, is not to become finished with it as quickly as possible, but rather to hold out in it as long as possible.

We have today become so pithless and weak-kneed that we are no longer able to hold out in the asking of a question. When the one philosophical medicine man cannot answer it, then one runs to the next. The demand increases the supply. In popular terms, this is called: an increased interest in philosophy.

Hermeneutics is itself not philosophy. It wishes only to place an object which has hitherto fallen into forgetfulness before today's philosophers for their "well-disposed consideration." That such minor matters are lost sight of today should not be surprising, given the great industry of philosophy where everything is geared merely to ensuring that one will not come too late for the "resurrection of metaphysics" which—so one has heard—is now beginning, where one knows only the single care of helping oneself and others to a friendship with the loving God which is as cheap as possible, as convenient as possible, and as profitably direct as possible into the bargain inasmuch as it is transacted through an intuition of essences.[2]

---

2. Remark added by H.: "No comparisons with foreign and dubious standards and frameworks, greater stress on its being something fundamental!"

Chapter Two

The Idea of Facticity and the Concept of "Man"[1]

In our indicative definition of the theme of hermeneutics, facticity = in each case our own Dasein in its being-there for a while at the particular time,[27] we avoided on principle the expression "human" Dasein or the "being of man."

The concepts of "man," namely, (1) a living being endowed with reason and (2) person or personhood, have arisen within experiencing and looking at contexts of objects in the world which were in each case given in advance in a definite manner. The first one belongs within a context of objects which is roughly indicated by the hierarchy of plants, animals, man, spirits, God. (Here we should not for the moment be thinking of the specific kind of experience found in the modern natural sciences and in modern biology in particular.) The second concept arose in the Christian explication of the original endowments of man as a creature of God, an explication which was guided by Revelation in the Old Testament. Both conceptual definitions are concerned with defining the items with which a thing, having been given in advance, comes to be furnished. A definite mode of being is subsequently ascribed to a pregiven thing, i.e., the latter is indifferently allowed to remain defined as a being-real.

Moreover, we should be wary of the concept of "a being endowed with reason," insofar as it does not capture the decisive meaning of ζῷον λόγον ἔχον [a living being which has discourse]. In the paragon academic philosophy of the Greeks (Aristotle), λόγος never means "reason," but rather discourse, conversation—thus man a being which has its world in the mode of something addressed.[2] This leveling off of concepts already came into play in the Stoics, and we find λόγος, σοφία [wisdom], and πίστις [belief] surfacing as hypostatic concepts in Hellenistic speculation and theosophy.

The concepts of man in circulation today go back to both above-mentioned sources, whether the idea of the person is picked up in connection with Kant and German Idealism or in relation to medieval theology.

§4. The concept of "man" in the biblical tradition

The explication of the idea of man as person, a concept incorporating the Greek notion of ζῷον λόγον ἔχον, was obtained by using as a guide a passage which has from different points of view been a classic one for

---

1. H.'s heading.
2. "summer semester 24 better" (remark added later by H.).

Christian theology, Genesis 1:26 in LXX (Septuagint): καὶ εἶπεν ὁ θεός· Ποιήσωμεν ἄνθρωπον κατ᾽ εἰκόνα ἡμετέραν καὶ καθ᾽ ὁμοίωσιν. ["And God said, 'Let us make man in our image and likeness.'"]* The words εἰκών [image] and ὁμοίωσις [likeness] are almost identical in meaning.

(The idea of God from looking at man—the respective [jeweiliger] religious state at the particular time. Seeing both points of view.) Cf. Kuhn: a sensory rational being (natura [nature], οὐσία [essence, being])—a "personal" being (ὑπόστασις [hypostasis], substantia [substance]), "capax alicujus veritatis de deo" ["capable of some truth about God"] et [and] "alicujus amoris dei" ["some love of God"] [Thomas Aquinas].³

The history of the interpretation of the Genesis passage begins with Paul, 1 Cor. 11:7: ἀνὴρ μὲν γὰρ οὐκ ὀφείλει κατακαλύπτεσθαι τὴν κεφαλήν, εἰκὼν καὶ δόξα θεοῦ ὑπάρχων. ["For a man ought not to cover his head, since he is the image and glory of God."]

Cf. 2 Cor. 3:18 and Rom. 8:29: ὅτι οὓς προέγνω, καὶ προώρισεν συμμόρφους τῆς εἰκόνος τοῦ υἱοῦ αὐτοῦ, εἰς τὸ εἶναι αὐτὸν πρωτότοκον ἐν πολλοῖς ἀδελφοῖς. ["For those whom he foreknew he also predestined to be conformed to the image of his Son, in order that he might be the first-born among many brethren."]

Problem: what is woman?

Tatian (circa 150), Λόγος πρὸς Ἕλληνας: μόνος δὲ ὁ ἄνθρωπος εἰκὼν καὶ ὁμοίωσις τοῦ θεοῦ, λέγω δὲ ἄνθρωπον οὐχὶ τὸν ὅμοια τοῖς ζῴοις πράττοντα ("not as ζῷον" [an animal]), ἀλλὰ τὸν πόρρω μὲν τῆς ἀνθρωπότητος πρὸς αὐτὸν δὲ τὸν θεὸν κεχωρηκότα ("rather as one having advanced further").⁴ Here both basic ways of considering man are clearly specified.

Augustine: Et dixit Deus, Faciamus hominem ad imaginem et similitudinem nostram. Et hic animadvertenda quaedam et conjunctio, et discretio animantium. Nam eodem die factum hominem dicit, quo bestias. Sunt enim simul omnia terrena animantia; et tamen propter excellentiam rationis, secundum quam ad imaginem Dei et similitudinem efficitur homo, separatim de illo dicitur, postquam de caeteris terrenis animantibus solite conclusum est, dicendo, Et vidit Deus quia bonum est. ["And God said, 'Let us make man in our image and likeness.' Here we should notice how the animals are grouped together and yet kept separate. Scripture says that man was made on the same day as the beasts, for they

3. Die christliche Lehre von der göttlichen Gnade, I. Theil (Tübingen, 1868), p. 11.

4. O. v. Gebhardt and A. Harnack (eds.), Texte und Untersuchungen zur Geschichte der altchristlichen Literatur, Vol. IV, No. 1 (Leipzig, 1888–93), Chap. 15 (68), p. 16, ll. 13–16. [Tatian, Oratio ad Graecos and Fragments, ed. and trans. Molly Whittaker (Oxford: Clarendon, 1982), p. 31 (modified): ". . . but man alone is the image and likeness of God. I mean by man not one who acts like the animals, but one who has advanced far beyond his humanity toward God himself."]

* Translations of biblical passages in this section are from The Holy Bible, Revised Standard Edition (Toronto: Wm. Collins Sons, 1971).

are all alike earthly animals. Yet on account of the excellence of reason, according to which man is made in the image and likeness of God, it speaks of him separately, after it had finished speaking of the other earthly animals in the customary manner, by saying, 'And God saw that it was good.'"][5] (In place of *Et factum est* ["And it was made"] and *et fecit Deus* ["and God made"]. Analogous: *Faciamus* ["Let us make"] — *Fiat* ["Let there be"].)[6]

Thomas Aquinas: *de fine sive termino productionis hominis prout dicitur factus ad imaginem et similitudinem Dei* ["on the end or term of man's production insofar as he is said to have been made in the image and likeness of God"].[7]

Quia, sicut Damascenus dicit, lib. 2 orth. Fid., cap. 12, a princ., homo factus ad imaginem *Dei dicitur, secundum quod per imaginem significatur* intellectuale, et arbitrio liberum, et per se potestativum, *postquam praedictum est de* ex-emplari, *scilicet* de Deo, *et de his quae processerunt ex divina potestate secundum ejus voluntatem, restat ut consideremus de ejus imagine, idest,* de homine: *secundum quod et ipse est suorum operum principium, quasi liberum arbitrium habens, et suorum operum potestatem.* ["Man is made in the *image* of God, and since this implies, so Damascene tells us (*De fide orthodoxa*, Bk. 2, Ch. 12), that he is *intelligent and free to judge and master of himself,* so then, now that we have agreed that *God* is the *exemplar cause* of things and that they issue from his power through his will, we go on to look at this image, that is to say, at *man* as the source of actions which are his own and fall under his responsibility and control."][8] This sentence bears within it the inner meth-odological structure of the major theological work of the Middle Ages.

Zwingli: *"ouch daß er {der mensch} sin ufsehen hat uf gott und sin wort, zeigt er klarlich an, daß er nach siner natur etwas gott näher anerborn, etwas mee nachschlägt, etwas züzugs zu jm hat, das alles on zwyfel allein darus flüßt, daß er nach der bildnuß gottes geschaffen ist.* [". . . in that he {man} also *looks up* to God and his Word, he shows clearly that in his nature he is born somewhat closer to God, is something more *after his stamp,* and has *something drawing* him to God — all this follows without a doubt from his having been created in the *image* of God."][9]

---

5. *De Genesi ad litteram imperfectus liber,* in Migne XXXIV (Paris, 1845), cap. 16, 55, p. 241. [*Saint Augustine on Genesis,* trans. Roland J. Teske (Washington, D.C.: Catholic University of America Press, 1991), pp. 182-83 (modified).]

6. Cf. *De Trinitate,* in Migne XLII (Paris, 1841), Liber XII, cap. 7, 12, p. 1004. [*The Trinity,* trans. Stephen McKenna (Washington, D.C.: Catholic University of America Press, 1963), pp. 353-55.]

7. *S. th.* (Parma edition) Ia, q. 93, prologus. [*Summa Theologiae,* Vol. 13, trans. Edmund Hill (New York: Blackfriars and McGraw-Hill, 1964), p. 49 (modified).]

8. *S. th.,* prologus to Ia-IIae (emphases in part by H.). [*Summa Theologiae,* Vol. 16, trans. Thomas Gilby (New York: Blackfriars and McGraw-Hill, 1969), p. 1 (modified).]

9. "Von Klarheit und gewüsse oder unbetrogliche des worts gottes," in *Werke,* Vol I: *Der deutschen Schriften erster Theil* (Zürich, 1828), p. 58 (H.'s emphases). ["Of the Clarity and Certainty or Power of the Word of God," in *The Library of Christian Classics,* Vol. 24: *Zwingli and Bullinger,* trans. G. W. Bromiley (London: SCM Press, 1953), p. 62 (modified).]

Calvin: *His praeclaris dotibus excelluit prima hominis conditio, ut ratio, intelligentia, prudentia, iudicium non modo ad terrenae vitae gubernationem suppeterent, sed quibus* transcenderent usque ad Deum *et aeternam felicitatem.* ["Man excelled in these noble endowments in his initial state, when reason, intelligence, prudence, and judgment not only sufficed for the government of his earthly life, but also enabled him *to ascend beyond even to God* and eternal happiness."][10]

From here the interpretation of personhood proceeds via German Idealism to Scheler.[11]

Scheler himself moves in a traditional fashion within ancient ways of posing questions which have become artificial—only the more disastrously by using the purified mode of seeing and explication in phenomenology.[12] He wants to define "the metaphysical position of man . . . within the whole of being, world, and God,"[13] the "genus *homo* [man]." He wants to do away with "the mythico-pictorial guise" of ideas and deal with the things themselves.[14]

In Scheler's distinction between the *"homo naturalis"*[15] [natural man] of natural science, "a unity of factual characteristics," of "a zoological species," and *homo historiae* [historical man], "the ideal unity in terms of which 'man' figures in the human sciences and in philosophy,"[16] the Kantian distinction—concept of nature and intelligible concept—simply gets watered down. ". . . an anthropologistic error,"[17] seen from the point of view of intentionality and eidetics. Everything "from the outside," "philosophy of things"!!

"What man is"—the meaning, being-with-a-view-to, hermeneutics of this question! He is "the intention and gesture of 'transcendence' itself,"[18] a God-seeker, "a 'between' { . . . } 'boundary.'" (Animal-God, both taken over), "a perpetual 'moving beyond',"[19] a "gateway"[20] for grace, ". . . the only meaningful idea of 'man' {is} the idea of an absolute *'theo-morphism,'*

10. *Institutio* I, 15, 8 (H.'s emphasis). [*Institutes of the Christian Religion*, Vol. 1, trans. Henry Beveridge (Grand Rapids, Mich.: Eerdmans, 1953), p. 169 (modified).]
11. See "Zur Idee des Menschen," 1st ed., in *Abhandlungen und Aufsätze*, Vol. I (Leipzig, 1915), pp. 319–67 (subsequently cited as "Zur Idee des Menschen"); the 4th ed. appeared in *Vom Umsturz der Werte. Abhandlungen und Aufsätze* in *Gesammelte Werke*, Vol. 3 (Bern, 1955), pp. 173–95. ["On the Idea of Man," trans. Clyde Nabe, *Journal of the British Society for Phenomenology* 9 (1978): 184–98.]
12. See p. 346/186 (here, as in the following, the first number gives the citation for the 1st ed., the second number the citation for the 4th ed.). ["On the Idea of Man," p. 192.]
13. Ibid., p. 319/173. ["On the Idea of Man," p. 184 (modified).]
14. Ibid., p. 320/173. ["On the Idea of Man," p. 184 (modified).]
15. Ibid., p. 322/174. ["On the Idea of Man," p. 185.]
16. Ibid., p. 323/175. ["On the Idea of Man," p. 185 (modified).]
17. Ibid., p. 321/173f. ["On the Idea of Man," p. 184.]
18. Ibid., p. 346/186. ["On the Idea of Man," p. 192.]
19. Ibid., p. 347f./186. ["On the Idea of Man," p. 192 (modified).]
20. Ibid., p. 348/187. ["On the Idea of Man," p. 193.]

the idea of an X which is a finite and living image of God, his likeness, his allegory—one of his infinitely many silhouettes on the great wall of being!"[21] Clear enough: a panorama! A picture, a story!

Ancient theology is haphazardly picked up and used by Scheler (cf. even Valentinian gnosis: σάρξ—ψυχή—πνεῦμα, *caro, anima, spiritus* [flesh, soul, spirit]), but whereas theologians in ancient times at least saw that it was a matter of theology, Scheler reverses everything and thereby ruins both theology and philosophy. This specific method of looking away from facticity is applied with great acumen in his book.

§5. *The theological concept of man and the concept of* "animal rationale"[1]

The thematic object of hermeneutics is in each case our own Dasein in its being-there for a while at the particular time[28]—insofar as it is interrogated with respect to, on the basis of, and with a view to the character of its being and the phenomenal structures of this being. Working thus from the point of view of a universal regional systematics, hermeneutics cuts out of this a certain domain for the purposes of a systematic investigation of it which is conducted in a specific manner.

In choosing a term to designate this region of being and appropriately demarcate it, we have avoided the expression "human Dasein," "human being," and will continue to do so. In all its traditional categorial forms, the concept of man fundamentally obstructs what we are supposed to bring into view as facticity. The question "What is man?" blocks its own view of what it is really after with an object foreign to it (cf. Jaspers).

Having been addressed as man, the beings-which-are-there in this kind of examination have already in advance been placed into definite categorial forms for investigating them, since one carries out the examination with the traditional definition *"animal rationale"* [rational animal] as a guide. Guided by this definition, the description has already prescribed a definite position for looking[29] at the these beings and has surrendered to it, failing to appropriate the original motives which led to it.

The concept of *animal rationale* was in fact already long ago uprooted from the soil of its original source and thus from the possibility of demonstrating it in a genuine manner.[2] Moreover, the development it underwent in modern philosophy (Kant) was determined by an interpretation of it in which motivating factors from Christian theology came into play. It is only from out of and on the basis of this situation that the

---

21. Ibid., p. 349/187. ["On the Idea of Man," p. 193 (modified).]

1. H.'s heading: "Additional Remarks on p. 4 [of the manuscript]. The Idea of Facticity and the Concept of Man." §5 (up to p. 24) was not delivered in the course.

2. Cf. Aristotle, *Nic. Eth.* A 6.

meaning of ideas of humanity, personhood, being-a-person can be under-stood—i.e., as certain formalizing detheologizations [*Entheologisierungen*]. Cf. Kant, *Religion within the Limits of Reason Alone* (1793).[3]

Scheler so little understands Kant's basic approach to the idea of person that in characterizing his notion of the feeling of respect merely as an "odd exception"[4] in his position he is unwilling to see that his own idea of person is distinguished from Kant's only insofar as it is more dogmatic and allows the borders between philosophy and theology to become even more blurred, i.e., ruins theology and undermines philos-ophy and its distinctive possibilities of critical questioning.

When Scheler defines man as an "intention and gesture of 'trans-cendence' itself," as a "God-seeker,"[5] this does not basically differ from Kant's notion of "having respect for" as being-open for the Ought as the moral law's mode of being-encountered.

The extent to which Scheler creates confusion in these basic starting points manifests itself *inter alia* in the fact that his idea of person is, right down to its linguistic formulation, exactly the one which the Reformation helped to bring to the fore in opposition to the superficial Aristotelianism of Scholasticism, cf. Zwingli, Calvin. Only that in the process what gets overlooked again is that here, i.e., in theology, man's various states, modes of being, must in principle be distinguished (*status integritatis, status corruptionis, status gratiae, status gloriae*) [state of purity, state of corruption, state of grace, state of glory] and that one cannot arbitrarily exchange one for the other.

When Scheler says that "it is Luther . . . who first defines him {man} explicitly as '*caro*' (flesh),"[6] it should be noted that he here confuses Luther with the prophet Isaiah (40:6). See Luther: *Porro caro significat totum hominem, cum ratione et omnibus naturalibus donis.* ["Flesh means further the whole man with his reason and all his natural endow-ments."][7] This flesh is in a *status corruptionis* which is from the start fully defined: to it belongs *ignorantia Dei, securitas, incredulitas, odium erga Deum* [ignorance of God, security, incredulity, enmity toward God], a de-

3. *Sämmtliche Werke*, Vol. 6, ed. G. Hartenstein (Leipzig, 1868), p. 120. [*Religion within the Limits of Reason Alone*, trans. Theodore M. Greene and Hoyt H. Hudson (Chicago: Open Court, 1960), pp. 21–22.]

4. *Der Formalismus in der Ethik und die materiale Wertethik*, in *Jahrbuch für Philosophie und phänomenologische Forschung* 2 (1916): 266. [*Formalism in Ethics and Non-Formal Ethics of Values: A New Attempt toward the Foundation of an Ethical Personalism*, trans. Manfred S. Frings and Roger L. Funk (Evanston: Northwestern University Press, 1973), p. 241 (modified).]

5. "Zur Idee des Menschen," p. 346/186. ["On the Idea of Man," p. 192.]

6. Ibid., p. 325/176 (H.'s emphasis). ["On the Idea of Man," p. 186.]

7. *In Esaiam Prophetam Scholia praelectionibus collecta, multis in locis non parva accessione aucta* (1534), cap. 40, in *Werke* (Erlangen edition), *Exegetica opera latina* XXII, ed. H. Schmidt (Erlangen and Frankfurt, 1860), p. 318. [*Luther's Works*, Vol. 17: *Lectures on Isaiah*, ed. Hilton C. Oswald (St. Louis: Concordia, 1972), p. 12 (modified).]

finitively negative relation to God in which man stands against God. *This* is as such *constitutive*!

The position which looked at man with the definition *"animal rationale"* as its guide saw him in the sphere of other beings-which-are-there with him in the mode of life (plants, animals) and indeed as a being which has language (λόγον ἔχον), which addresses and discusses its world — a world initially there for it in the dealings it goes about in its πρᾶξις [praxis], its *concern* taken in a broad sense. The later definition *"animal rationale,"* "rational animal," which was indifferently understood simply in terms of the literal sense of the words, covered up the intuition which was the soil out of which this definition of human being originally arose.

And within the developing self-understanding and consciousness of Christian Dasein, this propositional definition and its basic thesis became the now no longer discussed foundation for the theological definition of the idea of man out of which the idea of person developed (rational = is capable of knowing). This theological definition could be actualized only by being cut to the measure of its principle of knowledge, i.e., only with reference to Revelation, primarily Scripture. The guide taken from this was Genesis 1:26: καὶ εἶπεν ὁ θεός· Ποιήσωμεν ἄνθρωπον κατ' εἰκόνα ἡμετέραν καὶ καθ' ὁμοίωσιν. Human being was, in a manner cut to the measure of faith, defined in advance as being-created in the image of God. Apart from the Greek definition it externally adopted and rendered superficial, the Christian definition of the essence of human being is dependent on the idea of God which was added to the Greek definition and made normative for it.

Furthermore: for faith, man is in just such a manner as he happens to be encountered and now is, as "fallen" or as one redeemed and restored through Christ. Being-fallen, being-sinful, is not a state derived from God, but rather one into which man has brought himself. Accordingly, he must originally, as created by *God*, be good, and yet in such a way that in this being-in-such-a-manner (*bonum*) the possibility of falling is co-given. The formation of the state which the believer is now in is itself motivated from out of the respective [*jeweiligen*] primordial experience of being-sinful at the particular time, and for its part this experience is motivated from out of the respective primordiality or, alternately, nonprimordiality of the relation to God at the particular time.

This closed context of experience is the basis on which the anthropology of Christian theology has always stood and with which it has modified itself at particular times [*jeweilig*].

In the modern philosophical idea of being-a-person, the God-relation constitutive for the being of man is neutralized into a consciousness of norms and values as such. "Ego-pole" as such a primordial act-foundation, center of acts (ἀρχή [origin]).

If fundamental definitions of human being which are dogmatically theological are to be excluded in radical philosophical reflection on human being (it is not just this but rather the positively ontological problematic which is hindered by this approach, insofar as it already has an answer), then we must refrain from an explicit and especially a hidden, *inexplicit* orientation to already defined ideas of human being.

In being defined with the terms "our own," "appropriation," "appropriated,"[30] the concept of facticity—Dasein which is in each case our *own*—initially contains nothing of the ideas of "ego," person, ego-pole, center of acts. Even the concept of the self is, when employed here, not to be taken as something having its origin in an "ego"! (Cf. intentionality and its ἀρχή.)

§6. Facticity as the being-there of Dasein in the awhileness of temporal particularity. The "today"[1]

The theme of this investigation is facticity, i.e., our own Dasein insofar as it is interrogated with respect to, on the basis of, and with a view to the character of its being. It is all-important that the initial approach to this "object" of hermeneutical explication does not already in advance, and this means once and for all, lose sight of it. It is necessary to hold fast to the directive [*Weisung*] which is in advance co-given in the concept of facticity as the possible direction of filling it out. The being-there of our own Dasein is what it is precisely and only in its *temporally particular* "*there*," its being "*there*" *for a while*.[31]

A defining feature of the awhileness of temporal particularity is the *today*—in each case whiling, tarrying for a while, in the present, in each case our own present.[32] (Dasein as historical Dasein, its present. Being "in" the world, being lived "from out of"[33] the world—the present-everyday.)

The initial approach of interpretation sees itself to be referred [*verwiesen*] by its thematic object itself to the definite today in question. Not only is it the case that this reference must not be slackened off, but the possibility of getting a grasp of facticity depends on the degree of primordiality with which the reference is taken up and followed through to the end. Specific categories of Dasein need to be brought into view in its public manner of having-been-interpreted in the today, and to be able to do this we need to be wide-awake for them. The today ontologically: *the present of those initial givens which are closest to us*, every-one, being-with-each-other—"our time."

The reference to the today can be slackened off and turned into a fundamental *misunderstanding* in two ways. (1) For a start, if genuinely

---

1. H.'s heading: "Hermeneutics of the Situation."

following the reference were sought by attempting to get a grasp of the today hermeneutically through wide-ranging and longwinded discussions which provide entertaining *portraits* of the so-called "most interesting tendencies" of the present. (2) Moreover, if in this reference to the Dasein which is in each case our own a directive was heard to become zealously, though at bottom comfortably, fixated on vacantly *brooding* over an isolated ego-like self. Both curious in a worldly manner, culture and self-world.

What the above reference comes to is hermeneutical explication, not a report about "what's going on" in the world. "Today," in our day, i.e., everydayness, absorption, into the world, speaking from out of and on the basis of it, concern. Neither of the above-mentioned possibilities of going wrong in the very starting point of the analysis is merely accidental—rather they are constantly there as the analysis travels along its proper path. The execution of hermeneutics must constantly struggle against the possibility of getting sidetracked in these two ways.

Strong impulses for the hermeneutical explication presented here stem from the work of Kierkegaard. But his presuppositions, approach, manner of execution, and goal were fundamentally different, insofar as he made these too easy for himself. What was basically in question for him was nothing but the kind of personal reflection he pursued. He was a theologian and stood within the realm of faith, in principle outside of philosophy. The situation today is a different one.

What is crucial is that the today be lifted up into the starting point of analysis in such a manner that a *characteristic of being* already becomes visible in it. This characteristic then needs to be made transparent and as such moved up into the phenomenal sphere of facticity. And only then can we pose the obvious question of whether the "today" has accurately been hit upon in this characteristic of being which has been grasped in the starting point of the analysis.

The "today" can be fully defined in its ontological character as a how of facticity (existence) only when we have explicitly made visible the fundamental phenomenon of facticity: *"temporality"* (not a category, but an existential).

In anticipation of what will be said later about it, the following can be defined for the time being: The being-there of Dasein has its *open space of publicness*[34] and its ways of seeing there. It moves (a basic phenomenon) around in a definite mode of discourse about itself: *talk* (technical term). This discourse "about" itself is the public and average manner in which Dasein takes itself in hand, holds onto itself, and preserves itself. What lies in this talk is a definite comprehension which Dasein in advance has of itself: the guiding *"as what"* in terms of which it addresses "itself." This talk is thus the how in which a definite manner of Dasein's *having-been-interpreted* stands at its disposal. This being-interpreted is not something which would have been added to Dasein, externally applied to it, affixed to it, but rather something into which it has come of itself, from out of which it lives, on the basis of which it is *lived* (a how of its being).[2]

This being-interpreted in the today is further characterized by the fact that it is in fact not explicitly experienced, not explicitly present, it is a how of Dasein from out which and on the basis of which the Dasein of each is lived. Precisely because it makes up the open space of publicness and as such that *averageness* in which each can easily follow along, be involved, and be at home there, nothing which happens eludes it. The talk discusses everything with a peculiar insensitivity to difference. As this kind of averageness, the innocuous initial "givens" of the day which are closest to us and these givens as a for-the-most-part and for-most-of-us,[35] publicness is the mode of being of the *"every-one"*[36]: everyone says that . . . , everyone has heard that . . . , everyone tells it like . . . , everyone thinks that . . . , everyone expects that . . . , everyone is in favor of. . . . The talk in circulation belongs to no one, no one takes responsibility for it, every-one has said it.

"One" even writes books on the basis of such hearsay. This "every-one" is precisely *the* "no-one"[37] which circulates in factical Dasein and haunts it like a specter, a how of the fateful undoing of facticity to which the factical life of each pays tribute.

Fluent in all matters, Dasein's being-interpreted circumscribes the terrain on the basis of which Dasein can raise questions and make claims. It is what gives to the "there" of the factical being-there of Dasein [*Da-sein*] its characteristic of being-oriented in a definite manner, of a definite circumscription of the kind of sight possible for it and of its scope. Dasein speaks about itself and sees itself in such and such a manner, and yet this is only a *mask* which it holds up before itself in order not to be frightened by itself. The warding off "of" anxiety. Such visibility is the mask in which factical Dasein lets itself be encountered, in which it comes forth and appears before itself as though it really "were" it—in this masquerade of the public manner of being-interpreted, Dasein makes itself present and puts itself forward as the *height of living* (i.e., of industriousness).

An example: At a critical time when he was searching for his own Dasein, Vincent van Gogh wrote to his brother: "I would rather die a natural death than be prepared for it at the university. . . ."[3] This is not said here so as to give greater sanction to the moaning heard everywhere about the inadequacy of academic disciplines today. Rather, we want to ask: And what happened? He worked, drew the pictures in his paintings

2. Crossed out by H. with the remark "too soon."

3. Letter of October 15, 1879, in V. van Gogh, *Briefe an seinen Bruder*, ed. J. van Gogh-Bonger, trans. L. Klein-Diepold, Vol. I (Berlin, 1914), p. 157. [*The Complete Letters of Vincent van Gogh*, Vol. 1 (Greenwich, Conn.: New York Graphic Society, 1959), p. 192.]

from the depths of his heart and soul, and went mad in the course of this intense confrontation with his own Dasein.

Today: The situation of academic disciplines and the university has become even more questionable. What happens? Nothing. Everyone writes "brochures" on the crisis in academic disciplines, on the academic calling. The one says to the other: everyone's saying—as everyone's heard—academic disciplines have had it. Today there is already even a specialized body of literature on the question of how matters should be. Nothing else happens.

An example of an exponent of being-interpreted in the today is the *educated consciousness* of a time, *the talk heard in the public realm from the average educated mind*—today: the modern "mind." It lives off definite modes of interpreting. In the following what will be brought into relief as two such modes is: (1) historical consciousness (cultural consciousness), (2) philosophical consciousness.

Chapter Three

Being-Interpreted in Today's Today

The initial public givens of being-interpreted which are closest to us in the today will be seized upon in such a manner that by stepping back from this starting point and interpretively explicating it a *characteristic of the being* of facticity is able to come into our grasp. Having been grasped in this manner, this characteristic of being then needs to be developed into a concept, i.e., made transparent as an existential, so that a preliminary ontological access to facticity can thereby be worked out.[1]

Being-interpreted in the today can be investigated by pursuing two directions of interpretation there. These may be described as (1) historical consciousness in the today, (2) philosophy in the today.

Dominance of the direction of interpretation, the hermeneutical *how* therein (Not attitudes, a typology of views, in order to be able to see everything there is to be seen, no psychology of philosophy. Rather in order to be able to see in them how our Dasein *is*, our Dasein today, and indeed see it with regard to *modes of its being*, categorially, and in "holding" to Dasein, to consult it about whether this tendency of interpretation brings Dasein into view—whether this is at all ontology and what kind.)

§7. *Historical consciousness as an exponent of being-interpreted in the today*

Taking historical consciousness to be an exponent of being-interpreted in the today draws its motivation from the following criterion. The manner in which a time (the today which is in each case for a while at the particular time)[38] sees and addresses the past (either its own past Dasein or some other past Dasein), holding onto it and preserving it or abandoning it, is a sign of how a present stands regarding itself, how it as a being-there *is* in its "there." This criterion is itself only a certain expression of a fundamental characteristic of facticity, its temporality.

The kind of position which our today has regarding the past shows itself in the *historical human sciences*. These disciplines make themselves present and put themselves forward as the form of the path on which historical experience makes past life accessible—indeed, they give the leading directives for the manner in which what is past is to be objectified

---

1. H.'s n. on this paragraph: "Accurate regarding subject matter, but quite mistaken regarding method because too complicated and without a positive prospect."

in scientific theory. They hand over the historical past as a finished and readily available possession—characterized in terms of its basic look which has been apprehended in a definite manner and discussed from definite points of view—to the "educated consciousness" of the day (a how of the public manner of being-interpreted). The past, past life, as a scientific domain of objects.

As what is now past Dasein being grasped in advance in these disciplines? As having what character is it there for them as an object? Art, literature, religion, morals, society, science, and economy stand within an anticipatory characterization which runs in advance of, prepares a path for, and guides all particular instances of concretely interrogating and defining them: they are being encountered as "expression," as objectifications of the subjective, of the life of a culture (*the soul of a culture*) which presses forth into form in these objectifications.[2]

The pervasive uniformity in which this life of a culture comes to expression, holding itself therein, lingering for a time, and then becoming antiquated, is defined as the temporally particular [*jeweilige*] *style* of the culture. That these disciplines do not further investigate the character of being belonging to that of which cultural forms are supposed to be expressions shows clearly the extent to which their interests in understanding are aimed at forms of expression as such in the how of their expressive being. The one and only definition of the being of that which comes to expression in cultural forms is: a culture is an *organism*, an autonomous organic life (emerging, blossoming, dying out).

Spengler has provided a consequential and preeminent expression of this manner of seeing the past.[3] The sterile excitement of past philosophy and specialized branches of learning has long ago fallen silent. Since then, everyone has been secretly at work "capitalizing on it" from all angles— even in theology. Nietzsche, Dilthey, Bergson, the Vienna school of the history of art (Karl Lamprecht) have to be sure done preliminary work. But the important thing is that Spengler has made real headway in all these lines of thought which moved only uncertainly and with much anxiety toward a conclusion. No one prior to Spengler had the courage to actualize, without regard for consequences, the definitive possibilities found in the origin and development of modern historical consciousness.

One should not overlook the "new" step taken. Everything unproductive and halfhearted, all the dilettantism in fundamental issues and in conceptual habitus, should not obscure for us his pure diagnostic gaze.

2. H.'s n. on this paragraph: "The whole thing too psychological—instead also make visible the mode of temporal being, the mode of being-in, and the dominant ontology."

3. *Der Untergang des Abendlandes. Umrisse einer Morphologie der Weltgeschichte*, Vol. I: *Gestalt und Wirklichkeit* (Munich, 1920). [*The Decline of the West*, 1-vol. ed., trans. Charles Francis Atkinson (London: George Allen & Unwin, 1932).]

Effective forces which survive professional philosophy, the despondence of its stilted empty refinements. He has sensed what is going on. The others act as if everything were in the best order.

The next question is: having been objectified in such a manner as something which becomes form and has the being of expressions, in what mode does the past then become a task of theoretical knowledge (science), and what kind of task is this supposed to be? As a closed organism with its own life, a culture (multiplicity of such cultures) stands on its own. In this multiplicity of cultures which surge forth from tradition and within a definite interpretation, each one is in accord with the character of its ownmost being *put on a par* with all the others (like plants). In terms of its being, no past Dasein has priority over any other. Like the one culture, the others must also be presented.

Thus what is necessarily co-given from out of the character of the being of the past when it is seen in such a manner as an object is the *universality* of historical observation. Not the least motivation or justification can be derived from out of the object itself for myopically limiting ourselves to a single culture and conducting research on it alone. Accordingly, the field of objects for historical observation is broadened so that the "becoming of *all* humanity"[4] can be pursued in it.

When the past becomes an object in such a manner, what mode of theoretically understanding it, explicating it, and conceptually developing it now arises out of its kind of being and from the kind of object which it is?

It is no accident that today among the historical human sciences *history of art* has undergone the most development and that the other disciplines have the tendency to imitate it when possible.

The point of view into which each culture is being placed, the *with-respect-to-which and on-the-basis-of-which of seeing it and its looking the way it does*,[39] is the temporally particular how of the expressive being of its formation—each culture is interrogated with respect to and on the basis of its *style*, i.e., its forms of expression are traced back to a fundamental form of "soul and humanity." (The unity of its being-in-such-a-manner—is called?) Here the mode in which theoretical explications of what is past are carried out consists in bringing into relief the characteristics of the forms of form-endowed cultures—*morphology*.

What is being encountered in the past on the basis of the above ontological starting point is a multiplicity of cultures which are in themselves ontically on a par with each other, and this means that what is appropriate for this context of objects is that morphological observation should be seen through to the end. The multiplicity must itself be inter-

---

4. Ibid., p. 218. [*The Decline of the West*, p. 159 (modified).]

rogated with respect to and on the basis of its being endowed with form, it itself still needs to be made accessible in terms of form. The one culture has to be held up against the other with an eye to form. It is in this manner that the method of *universally comparing forms* arises. Here the relational categories of homology, analogy, synchronism, parallelism come into play.

The totality of the historical past which is seen and explicated in such a manner becomes condensed into a closed form-endowed context of forms (i.e., it can become so condensed — *condensation,* able to be mastered at a glance, running a set course). It becomes graspable in charts and under rubrics in which the paths on which comparisons can be made have been laid down and fixed in an orderly manner.

Preparing a path of research in advance, the guiding anticipatory apprehension of the character of the object, the "past," as something consisting of stylistically unified forms of expression which belong in each case to temporally particular and autonomous cultures motivates — not only from out of this domain of objects as seen in such a manner, but also from out of the appropriate stance for accessing it — a definite mode of historical explication: *classifying which compares forms.* (Classification — grasping forms. (1) Classification, (2) classification and, with sharper focus, the idea of culture in general — consequences — opposite pole.)[40]

Spengler has drawn up the consequential program in an all-encompassing manner: "Before my eyes there emerges a specifically Western method of superlative historical research, one which has never appeared before and necessarily remains foreign to the classical soul and to every other soul but ours. A comprehensive physiognomic of all Dasein, a morphology of the becoming of *all* humanity which drives onward along its path to the highest and last ideas — the duty of penetrating the world-feeling not only of our own soul, but of *all* souls whatsoever in which grand possibilities have until now appeared, individual grand cultures being their embodiment in the field of actuality. This philosophical point of view to which we have been elevated and to which we are entitled in virtue of our analytical mathematics, contrapuntal music, and perspective painting presupposes — in that its scope far transcends the talents of the systematist — the eye of an artist and indeed an artist who can feel the whole sensible and tangible world around him dissolve completely into a deep infinity of mysterious relations. So Dante felt, so Goethe felt."[5]

(Subsequent application to history in the usual sense. History of religion, etc. Circuitously reported and talked about without having a relation to it.)

---

5. Ibid., p. 218f. (emphases in part by H.). [*The Decline of the West,* p. 159 (modified).]

§8. Today's philosophy as an exponent
of being-interpreted in the today

A second exponent of *being-interpreted in the today* can be found in the *philosophy* of today. Taking philosophy to be a mode of interpretation of factical Dasein is based on a certain formal characteristic of traditional philosophy itself. Its traditional tendency can be described in empty generality: it sets itself the task of defining the *totality of beings* in its different regions, the respective kinds of consciousness of these regions, and the overarching unity of both of these in ultimate foundations (principles).

Even the Dasein of life must fall within the compass of this thematic field of inquiry as so defined in formal terms. The traditional philosophical disciplines of ethics, philosophy of history, psychology are always turning "discourse" to life in some manner. Questioning with respect to it is inexplicitly there in them, more or less secured in their foundations. In the traditionally posed questions of these disciplines, what is also more or less explicitly interrogated is human life, and this is being done within some point of view from which life is seen. Accordingly, we should be able hermeneutically to read off from such philosophy *what* it is grasping the Dasein of life *as* in advance, how "the talk" about Dasein is circulating in it, how, that is to say, discourse is proceeding in it insofar as it is a definite mode in which a time is speaking about itself—its being-there.

What our analysis comes to is solely this hermeneutical assessment. It is not a matter of entering into a debate with this philosophy or indeed refuting it. Providing a sprawling picture of its main "currents" is not only of no importance here but a distraction from the sole question before us: into which guiding point of view has philosophy's domain of objects been placed?

The theme of philosophy is the universal, the one and only *totality of beings* which includes everything and makes of it a unity. Insofar as a multiplicity of regions, levels, and gradations of being comes to be encountered, there arises vis-à-vis it the task of a system which can encompass it and which as such includes two tasks: first, sketching out the conceptual framework, the basic guidelines, of the context of classification, and then allocating[1] the respective places for concrete beings in the various domains of the system.

In this kind of treatment of the totality of beings, classificatory relations as such, relations of priority as such, organization into levels as such, and relations of difference and sameness as such take on a distinctive character. *The relational* as such pushes to the fore and becomes the

---

1. H.'s n.: "too soon."

object proper. Insofar as it dominates and pervades everything, it constitutes being in the authentic sense. The classificatory dimension is what is properly immutable in itself, something elevated above that which it organizes and rules, the *trans-temporal in-itself*, trans-temporal being, validity, value, subsistence (in contrast to "sensible reality").

This context of being or validity is either taken to be something free-floating, absolutely valid in itself, or characterized as being *both* what is thought by an Absolute Spirit *and* its thinking—and the latter is in turn taken either in Hegel's sense or in that of Augustinian Neoplatonism.

Especially since they remain undefined and vague, these differences are not of decisive importance for the ontological character of what comes into view as an object within the above-mentioned guiding point of view or for the *how* of seeing it. The same applies to the following difference: the contexts of classification can be characterized in a uni-dimensional, shallow, and static manner within a Platonic approach, or they can be approached dialectically. Even *dialectic* requires, as the condition of its own possibility, the seeing-in-such-and-such-a-manner described above, i.e., seeing the totality of beings as something defined in advance in the sense of that which can be grasped and enclosed in a classificatory order. The most proper business of dialectic—a unifying which constantly sublates, *com*prehends, then reaches *out* again for something new—is conducted, as it were, at the expense of this initial approach to the possibility of classification.

The pertinacity of dialectic, which draws its motivation from a very definite source, is documented most clearly in Kierkegaard. In the properly philosophical aspect of his thought, he did not break free from Hegel. His later turn to Trendelenburg is only added documentation for how little radical he was in philosophy. He did not realize that Trendelenburg saw Aristotle through the lens of Hegel. His reading the Paradox into the New Testament and things Christian was simply negative Hegelianism. But what he really wanted (phenomenal) was something different. When today the attempt is made to connect the authentic fundamental tendency of phenomenology with dialectic, this is as if one wanted to mix fire and water.

In place of additional description of today's philosophy, we can let one of its self-explanations speak for itself: "All of us—Rickert, the phenomenologists, the movement associated with Dilthey—meet up with one another in the great struggle for *the timeless in the historical* or *beyond the historical*, for the *realm of meaning* and its historical expression in a concrete developed culture, for a *theory of values* which leads beyond the merely subjective toward the objective and the valid."[2]

2. E. Spranger, "Rickerts System," *Logos* 12 (1923–24): 198 (emphases in part by H.).

The authentic tendency of Dilthey's thought is not the one cited above. As for the "phenomenologists," I ask to be exempted.

"Toward the objective" is explained as "away from the merely subjective." This philosophy—one could describe it as the "Platonism of barbarians"[3]—thinks itself to be in a secure position vis-à-vis historical consciousness and the historical itself. From this position, it denounces the attempt to keep philosophy within history as historicism. Thus the one exponent of being-interpreted (philosophy) stands in opposition to the other (historical consciousness) and claims to overcome it. This disagreement is *the* public problem within today's being-interpreted: "All of us. . . ."

Symptomatic of this drive toward the objective is the rejection of the reflections of epistemology and philosophy of science, the grand gesture now commonplace among philosophers of history: objective metaphysics. An unmistakable sign of the pull in this direction is how and where everyone seeks counsel in the history of philosophy. Aristotle (as traditionally interpreted), Leibniz, and Hegel have become the models. The direction of philosophical interpretation today holds itself fast within its starting point in a universal context of being which is able to be defined through the *universal classification* appropriate to it. The basic comportment of historical consciousness has likewise shown itself to be classification which compares forms.

(What kind of being stands in forehaving here? Being-available, being-present, cultural transformation and variation which are present. Forehaving, foreconception: defining = making visible in overview.)

§9. Insert: "Dialectic"[1] and phenomenology

The tendency of today's philosophy was described above as the "Platonism of barbarians"—it is "barbarian" because the authentic roots of Plato's thought are missing. The original situation in which Plato carried out his mode of questioning, setting up starting points, and making claims to knowledge was forfeited long ago and never again attained. Heterogeneous motives have entered into today's philosophical speculation, and they are, moreover, never examined with regard to their historical provenance. A characteristic passage regarding what we are dealing with here: Plato, *Politeia* VI 511b-c.[2] The decisive dimension of the initial approach to the object of philosophy can be read off from this passage.

---

3. See Plato, *Politeia*, ed. Burnet (Oxford, 1906), VI 511b-c. [*The Collected Dialogues of Plato*, p. 746.]
   1. H.'s heading.
   2. Cf. n. 3 in §8.

As something opposed to static juxtaposition (e.g., that found even in phenomenology), dialectic has its source in the same error committed by that which it wishes to remedy. It steps into an already constructed context, though there really is no context here, i.e., what is missing is the radical fundamental looking in the direction of and at the *object of philosophy* from out of which and on the basis of which even the how of what is understood emerges in its "unity." What develops unity is not an external framework of classification and the "character of process" bound up with it, but the how of the respective [*jeweiligen*] understanding insofar as it has a direction which is decisive for each step along the way. Every category is an existential and *is* this as such, not merely in relation to other categories and on the basis of this relation.

Now to provide a fundamental orientation regarding dialectic insofar as an understanding of phenomenology is in question here. A formalistic answer which would have real relevance is impossible, just as any question of the relationship between these two can come up for discussion only if it is demanded by concrete research. Idle methodological programs ruin science.

Dialectic places itself in a position of superiority over phenomenology from two related points of view, both of which have to do with the dignity of the knowledge it purportedly attains.

1. Dialectic sees in phenomenology the stage of the most immediate immediacy of grasping. This immediacy can only become acquainted [be*kannt*] with something—knowing [Er*kennen*] remains beyond its reach, i.e., it does not attain the higher kind of immediacy, i.e., mediated immediacy. The best it can do is to define the *appearance* of Spirit in its first stage—the authentic being of Spirit in its self-knowing remains closed off to it.

2. Moreover: owing to its higher authentic possibility of knowledge, dialectic alone succeeds in penetrating the irrational, and if not completely, then nonetheless more so than in phenomenology—the irrational, something spoken of at the same time as the transcendent and the metaphysical.

It's true: phenomenology is the stage of immediate knowledge—if, that is, one grasps phenomenology from the point of view of dialectic. And the question is whether a primordial understanding of phenomenology can ever be gained in this manner. One already presupposes dialectic. Nothing can be decided on this level of posing questions.

This also needs to be said: In fact, there is in phenomenology a *limit* placed on knowing, or rather a possibility of doing this, one which is not always seized upon and perhaps not at all today. Be this as it may, the question is whether such a limit in the meaning of the basic tasks of philosophy is a defect on account of which phenomenology lags far behind dialectic's more lofty work of penetrating the depths, raising them to the level of knowledge, and then penetrating further into them.

And at the same time we need to ask: What does "irrational" mean? This term can in fact be defined only on the basis of an idea of rationality. And where does the definition of this idea come from? Granting for a moment this disastrous pair of concepts (form-content, finite-infinite) — if it turned out that the rationality and, correspondingly, the irrationality of the aesthetic, for example, were totally different from those of religion, i.e., if it turned out that the basic employment of the term "rational" was limited to something utterly empty of subject matter, what could this rationality ever achieve?

Can thematic objects ever be defined in this negative fashion as something irrational? When this approach is taken, one does not understand what one is doing—one fails to notice that all dialectic remains directionless when the decisive factor is not a definite fundamental looking in the direction of the *subject matter*, a fundamental rationality which constantly tests itself and proves itself by looking at the subject matter and not by means of dialectic as such.

For example, stressing that a dialectical system contains a richness of content concerning phenomena of life contributes so little to redefining the actual character of the being of dialectical comportment that it now only becomes all the more conspicuous in its "tendency to go wrong" precisely vis-à-vis the life which it is dealing with as an object.

Regarding what it procures in philosophy, all dialectic in fact always lives from the table of others. The shining example: Hegel's logic. That it simply assimilates and reworks the one traditional form of logic leaps into view after just a cursory examination. And not only this, but he himself expressly underscores it: "this traditional material," Plato, Aristotle, is "an extremely important source, indeed a necessary condition {and} presupposition to be gratefully acknowledged."[3] (In addition: when Hegel picked up his material, what state of interpretation was it in?)

Thus dialectic lacks radicality, i.e., is fundamentally unphilosophical, on two sides. It must live from hand to mouth and develops an impressive eloquence in dealing with this readymade material. If it gains acceptance, the burgeoning Hegelese will once again undermine even the possibility of having a mere sensitivity for philosophy. No accident that Brentano, from whom came the first impulses for the development of phenomenology, sensed in German Idealism the deepest ruin of philosophy. A year of reading and one can talk about everything, such that it really looks like something and the reader himself believes he's really got

---

3. G. W. F. Hegel, *Wissenschaft der Logik, 1. Teil,* ed. G. Lasson (Leipzig, 1923), 2d preface, p. 9. [*Hegel's Science of Logic,* trans. A. V. Miller (London: George Allen & Unwin, 1969), p. 31 (modified).]

something. One ought to have a close look at the sophistry being pursued today with schemata like form-content, rational-irrational, finite-infinite, mediated-unmediated, subject-object.

It is what the critical stance of phenomenology ultimately struggles against. When the attempt is made to unify them, one treats phenomenology in a superficial manner. Phenomenology can only be appropriated phenomenologically, i.e., only through *demonstration* and not in such a way that one repeats propositions, takes over fundamental principles, or subscribes to academic dogmas.

A large measure of critique is initially required for this, and nothing is more dangerous than the naive *trust in evidence* exhibited by followers and fellow travelers. If it is the case that our relation to the things themselves in seeing is the decisive factor, it is equally the case that we are frequently deceived about them and that the possibility of such deception stubbornly persists. Perhaps called once to be the conscience of philosophy, it has wound up as a pimp for the public whoring of the mind, *fornicatio spiritus* [fornication of the spirit] (Luther).

The upshot of these observations is: The question of the relation between dialectic and phenomenology must be decided vis-à-vis the *object* of philosophy—and more precisely within the fundamental task of concretely working out the question of this object and how to decide it. But dialectic sets itself on the sideline regarding this task. It cannot hold out in such a thing as staying with the object and allowing it to prescribe the right mode of grasping it and the limits to this. (The question of the object of philosophy is not formalistic preliminary reflection, idle dilettantism. Cf. "Introduction," 21–22.[4])[41]

§10. A look at the course of interpretation[1]

Our theme is Dasein in its being-there for a while at the particular time.[42] And our task: to bring this into view, have a look at it, and understand it in such a manner that in it itself basic characteristics of its being are able to be brought into relief. Dasein is not a "thing" like a piece of wood nor such a thing as a plant—nor does it consist of experiences, and still less is it a subject (an ego) standing over against objects (which are not the ego). It is a distinctive being [*Seiendes*] which precisely insofar as it "is there" for itself in an authentic manner is not an object—in formal terms: the toward-which of a being-directed toward it by mean-ing it. It is an object insofar as it becomes a theme of *observation*, but this says nothing

---

4. H.'s lecture course in the winter semester of 1921–22, *Phänomenologische Interpretationen zu Aristoteles* (*Gesamtausgabe*, Vol. 61), which he always cited as "Introduction."
    1. H.'s heading: "regarding p. 9 [of the manuscript] — recap."

as to whether it must also be an object for the kind of experience in which it is *there* for itself and in which analysis of it actualizes itself in an authentic manner.

(It is not a matter of obtaining and delivering a series of propositions and dogmas about this Dasein, generating a philosophy around it, about it, and with it, or, as is the main concern for most today, staging a new direction in phenomenology and increasing still more the noise and industry of philosophy which already looks suspicious enough.)[2]

This special investigation is being conducted with a view to working out concretely the right direction of looking toward the genuine phenomenon. For this, it is important that we already see it in its peculiar character there where everyone least suspects.

There for a while at the particular time, Dasein is there in the awhileness of temporal particularity. This awhileness is co-defined by the particular today of Dasein, its being today for a while. The today is always today's today.[43] *A* mode in which the today makes itself present, in which therefore one already sees something like Dasein, is the *open space of publicness* which belongs to the being-there of Dasein. This publicness actualizes itself by passing around and sustaining definite kinds of discourse about . . . , opinions about. . . . The discourse circulates everywhere and about everything—in a characteristic fashion—and thus presumably also about what is after all not so very far from Dasein, namely, *itself.*

Accordingly, if the Dasein of today is to be brought into view from out of the initial givens of the today which are closest to us, we need to consult this talk which belongs to its publicness, in which it speaks especially of itself, in which it is thus there as an object in some manner. Such public talk, educated consciousness, always derives from more original modes of dealing with the matters discussed. Two such modes in which we find some form of discourse about Dasein are *inter alia* historical consciousness and philosophy—prominent and explicit modes of a speaking which in a distinctive manner speaks of itself.

In history and philosophy, Dasein is speaking about itself directly or indirectly, and this means that it has a comprehension of itself which it continues to work out in detail—it is there in these modes as having been interpreted in such and such a manner. These modes are themselves modes of interpreting.

Thus the Dasein of today is to be interrogated by interrogating today's historical consciousness and philosophy with respect to and on the basis of how Dasein is there in them and how it is comprehended in them. History and philosophy—as the today which is to be subjected to a

---

2. This paragraph crossed out by H.

destruction—seen here in a one-sided manner and with respect to the question of the being of Dasein.

It is initially a matter of simple assessments—in light of these the course of our descriptive interpretation is already sketched out in advance regarding its basic task: History and philosophy are modes of interpretation, something which Dasein itself is, in which it lives—and insofar as Dasein itself comes forth and appears in them, these modes which are in Dasein itself are modes of its having itself in a definite manner. These modes of Dasein are cut to the measure of Dasein—thus the genuine question of hermeneutics here turns out to be: *what characteristic of the being of Dasein* shows up in these modes of its having-itself?

Chapter Four

Analysis of Each Interpretation
Regarding Its Mode of Being-Related to Its Object

The hermeneutical question for which the horizon has now been provided is: *As what* is *factical Dasein* being encountered in these two directions of interpretation (historical consciousness and philosophy) and that means at the same time in its own dominant manner of being-interpreted? As what is it addressed in accord with the most immanent sense of these two directions of interpretation? Furthermore: in its being-interpreted, as what is factical Dasein grasping itself, as what does it have itself? And finally: what is the having-itself-there of Dasein's being-there[44] as being, as a how of facticity, an existential?

That what our portrayal and analysis of these two modes of Dasein's being-interpreted come to is solely the interpretive bringing into relief of a characteristic of the being of Dasein is something we need to hold fast to. Our portrayal of them is in itself already a first bringing into relief and indication of this characteristic of being, i.e., a formal directive to ontological seeing. And here we need to set aside the prejudice that an ontology of objects in nature or an ontology of cultural objects running parallel to it (ontology of things in nature and things in the mind) is the only kind of ontology or rather the one serving as the model for other kinds.

How are we to bring into view the *"as what"* with respect to and on the basis of which each of the two directions of interpretation comprehends its object? On the basis of a path of analysis in which we look to their particular *modes of being-related* to their object. Light can be shed on the tendency of this relation to . . . by illuminating and analyzing at the same time the mode of actualizing this relating-itself-to (see Husserl's *Logical Investigations!*).[1]

§11. The interpretation of Dasein in historical consciousness

The character of the object "the past" — the theme of *historical consciousness* — stands within a fundamental definition: something's *being-an-expression* of something. Thus characterized in its suchness by its being-an-expression, the context of the past's being-in-such-a-manner is subjected to a knowing and defining in which it is understood with respect to and on the basis of the temporally particular kinds of forms of expressive

---

1. Remark added by H.: "Sharper focus here on interpretation, being-in, care."

being which were once there for a while, i.e., on the basis of temporally particular *styles*. (What is past, no longer present—world as being-an-expression-of—and this: style. Looking in the direction of and at the style, having-it-in-view: fore-sight.)

The beings which are expressions of something demand of themselves that the proper mode of accessing and appropriating them lies in pursuing and observing the characteristics of *reference* (The term "reference" will later be assigned a special usage. Used improperly here.) found in these objects which have been defined in such a manner. An investigating which looks into defined contexts of representation and pursues them.

The expressive networks of reference, both those within a cultural system[2] and those extending from one cultural system to others, demand—in each case because of their multiplicity—the possibility that the preservation of them is able to hold onto them[45] in a *unified* manner—otherwise the object being expressed could not be obtained from them. The unified manner in which this preservation holds onto the expressed networks of reference (the context of being-in-such-a-manner) is based on the fact that in pursuing these networks, bringing them into relief, and defining them investigations are actualizing themselves from out of a *foresight* with respect to and having-in-view of style—a foresight with respect to . . . which pervades and dominates each step of the investigating. It is within this point of view which looks in the direction of and at style that interrogations of funds of historical facts with respect to the mode of their expressive being are actualized. These under*takings* [*Vornehmen*] are themselves motivated and developed in different ways.

This guiding point of view is constitutive for actualizing the fundamental work of research precisely there where one does not at all suspect: in the critical choice of sources and their first interpretation. This anticipatory having-present of the cultural object in terms of the characteristic of style, running in advance of all concrete sifting of sources and preparing the paths of looking required for this (e.g., declaring a source to be inauthentic or determining authorship or uncovering literary filiations), makes itself explicit only *in* its actualization.

The *anticipatory forehaving of the unity of style which prepares a path of research in advance* not only proves itself regarding its adequacy to its subject matter, but it thereby explicates itself for the first time with regard to the previously still hidden basic characteristics of style in the starting point. This anticipatory forehaving of style is characterized relationally by a *holding-in-view which observes,* and the concrete mode of gaining access to the context of being-in-such-a-manner and appropriating it by

---

2. An expression from Dilthey: religion, art, etc. [The German edition provides no explanation as to whether this note is Heidegger's or the editor's.]

an investigating which, in being led along the path of this observation, looks into and pursues the multiplicity of references. (Classifying as sojourn, abode, holding out, a how of temporal being, the present. Form—look—being-an-expression of—distinguishing feature.)

Historical consciousness now places itself in principle, i.e., on the basis of having in advance objectified and defined what is past as something which consists of expressive beings, before the total multiplicity of beings which are in such a manner. That is to say, corresponding to its ownmost relational tendency, historical understanding and defining demands of itself that it hold to and never depart from the above-mentioned stance of looking into and pursuing these beings in such a manner. An observing which looks into . . . as a certain "whiling" or "tarrying" among. . . .

This *tarrying* among . . . which becomes involved in all cultures and pursues them in a uniform manner is what sustains the possibility of actualizing a universal *classifying* which compares forms. In it lies the relational guarantee that each and every past cultural form has the same opportunity of being encountered in an *"objective"* manner. And the tarrying among all the multiplicities of forms on both levels is one which defines, i.e., compares, and as such compares in a universal manner. It is a constant looking here and there, seeing this and that. So long as it understands itself, this constant being-on-the-way of seeing will, so that it can do its work, never halt, make a sojourn, and hold out there.

What is being encountered in this tarrying as the universal possibility of expression which is in case subdivided into unities of style is what is past—it is beings in the how of their having-been, i.e., as *already there* for that tarrying among them which looks into them—availability of the past, a past present—not being-past as my, our virtuality.[3] (Technical term?)

The "already there" in the past, and indeed this "already there" in its vivid multiplicity of forms, is being encountered by the tarrying which sees it in a definite manner and looks toward its contexts of reference in such a way that a *pull* arises from it itself, from the content of the subject matter which has been defined in advance in it—a pull which constantly draws the tarrying which compares anew into the looking-into which becomes involved in and pursues, and it does this in such a manner that the looking-into must of itself hold itself in this pursuing and linger in it. (The pull: world, life, publicness, what was going on.)

Definite phenomenal characteristics have now come into relief: (1) looking in the direction of and at . . . , holding-in-view; (2) the investigating which looks into, pursues, and makes available the concrete

---

3. Remark added by H.: "Missing here is the kind of knowledge: ascertaining, taking cognizance of, portraying."

contexts of being; (3) this ascertaining as constantly led along by the above-mentioned looking in the direction of . . . ; (4) this observing which looks into . . . as a "whiling" or "tarrying" among . . . ; (5) this tarrying in its mode of actualization, i.e., a comparing which runs here and there, i.e., an abode-less tarrying which never halts, makes a sojourn, and holds out there (and yet it holds itself and sojourns in what it goes back to!); (6) the among-which of the tarrying as having the character of the "already there" of beings-which-have-been; (7) the pull arising from it, one which is such that it develops the tarrying into a *"must* tarry" on the basis of an autonomous tendency of grasping and recording.

These phenomenal characteristics should suffice for gaining a preliminary phenomenological understanding of historical consciousness in terms of the character of its relation-to and its actualizing of this relation. The phenomenon of being-nowhere found in the "must see everything" and indeed everything in the historical past may be defined terminologically as *curiosity which is led and pulled along,* i.e., led along by its object.

We have thematized historical consciousness as an exponent of Dasein's being-interpreted, as *a mode of the public being of life.* As a mode of interpretation, it even makes itself present and introduces itself to the public in the mode of its being, i.e., by interpreting itself. This means: Historical consciousness is "there" in such a fashion that it brings itself *into the open space of publicness with a definite self-interpretation,* holds itself in this publicness, lingers in it, pervades it, and thus dominates it. In this self-interpretation, it brings to language what it thinks it is all about and comes to, and it does this with respect to the Dasein of life itself. As a mode of interpretation of Dasein, its self-interpretation in the public realm will accordingly express what Dasein itself thinks *it* is all about and comes to. What this might be is something which needs to be brought to light from out of the self-interpretation of historical consciousness (and correspondingly from out of the self-interpretation of philosophizing).

Spengler underscores as a longstanding deficiency in historical observation and science that it has never achieved what it has in fact striven for: "to be *objective.*"[4] It will be objective only when it succeeds in "sketching out a picture of history which is not dependent on the contingent standpoint of the observer in his 'present.'"[5] What was achieved long ago in the natural sciences—a distance from the objects studied so that they can speak purely for themselves—has until now been lacking in the world of history. It is thus necessary to carry out "once again the deed of Copernicus"[6] for history, i.e., to free history from the perception

4. *Der Untergang des Abendlandes,* Vol. 1, Chap. 2, pp. 135ff. [*The Decline of the West,* pp. 93ff.]

5. Ibid., p. 135. [*The Decline of the West,* p. 93 (modified).]

6. Ibid., p. 136. [*The Decline of the West,* p. 94 (modified).]

and standpoint of the observer, "to remove history from the personal prejudices of the observer, which in our own case have made of it nothing more than a history of a partial past, one in which the contingent present of the European West is supposed to be the goal of history, and its public ideals and interests the criteria for determining both the achievements of the past and what ought to be achieved in the future—this is the aim of all that follows."[7]

In this self-interpretation, historical consciousness accordingly places itself before the task of gaining an overview of "the total fact of man,"[8] i.e., bringing human Dasein into view in an absolutely objective manner. A new task in the sense that a new and authentic possibility of Dasein and of grasping and recording Dasein (in an objective manner) is being offered.

This self-interpretation is not simply presenting historical consciousness such that it takes cognizance of itself and has knowledge about itself, but rather it is making it familiar with itself in such a manner that it pushes itself, i.e., its being-interpreted in the today, into the kind of tarrying in which the past is encountered in an unprejudiced objective manner. This self-interpretation itself moves toward the object it wants to grasp and record and toward the pull arising from it, i.e., in being pulled along, its curiosity is itself pushing itself in the direction of the pull.

In its self-presentation, this mode of interpretation *also* speaks *in favor of* the employment and maintenance of the Dasein which is seen in such a manner—an employment and maintenance which are to be actualized in it itself. In the objective distance of its approach to the past, this historical consciousness also has the *present* of Dasein before itself in an equally objective manner, and this means that it "already" has Dasein's *future* objectively before itself in accord with the character of the historical it initially put forth. The prediction and advance calculation of the future, the "decline of the West," is not a whim on Spengler's part or a cheap witticism for the masses, but rather the consequential expression of the fact that regarding its ownmost possibilities which have been prescribed for it, inauthentic historical consciousness has thought itself through to the end. (The not-yet, actually the present when it is *calculated*—reading it off and anticipating it by way of comparison.)

In making today's historical consciousness present and putting it forward, Spengler represents it precisely in the form in which it must understand itself in accord with its own possibilities. Opposition from specialists in specific fields of history is fundamentally of no consequence *when* they point out his misinterpretations or total neglect of relevant funds of historical facts (such misinterpretation and neglect are quite

---

7. Ibid., p. 136. [*The Decline of the West*, p. 94 (modified).]
8. This phrase is found only in later editions of Spengler's work. See p. 128 in the 1923 edition, as well as p. 126 in the 1969 reprint. [*The Decline of the West*, p. 93 (modified).]

important from a different point of view). If not explicitly, then in the basic principles of their approach, these specialists are coming more and more under Spengler's influence.

Hence when they offer opposition on basic issues, this only shows that they do not understand what they are doing, i.e., the historical human sciences are not aware that they mistakenly seize upon a very specific possibility of conducting research, i.e., history of art, i.e., that they are attempting to elevate themselves to a higher "intellectual" plane by imitating it, instead of each particular [jeweils] discipline focusing, as history of art itself does, on its own object, the character of its being, and the appropriate possibility of gaining access to it and defining it.

To imitate history of art is to misuse it, i.e., have little regard for it, i.e., misunderstand it. When the other human sciences imitate it, they understand it as little as they do themselves. (History of art—why genuine in this regard (style, form, expression)? Its object: also the "classifying"! Still a lack of clarity here, obvious what tasks lie ahead.)

Religion is misunderstood in the very core of its being-there when history of religion today buys into the cheap game of sketching out types, i.e., stylistic forms, of religiosity in entertaining illustrated charts. Analogous points need to be made about economic history, history of philosophy, and legal history. In their genuine character at particular times [jeweilig], these possibilities concretely come into being and are there not by having a cleverly thought-out philosophical system of cultural systems laid before them as a plan of operation, but rather only through the fact that at the particular time and respectively [jeweils] in "this" discipline the right man at the right place and at the right time steps in and takes hold of it in a decisive manner. (What philosophy should contribute to this—that is not something which needs to be "talked" about.)

§12. The interpretation of Dasein in philosophy

A corresponding analysis of the *second direction of interpretation, philosophy,* must now be carried out. This means: what must be defined is the guiding mode of being-related to its object which belongs to the comportment of philosophical knowing and, in unison with this, the *"as what"* in terms of which the theme of philosophy is there for it as an object. The mode of being-related to . . . will for its part become clear in an analysis of the character of philosophy's actualization of its comporting-itself toward . . . and its holding-itself in this comporting.

9. A remark clearly added later by H.
10. This sentence crossed out by H.

In the previous indicative characterization of this second exponent of being-interpreted in the today, attention should have been called to a certain difficulty. Not only does the multiplicity of divergent directions in philosophy today make it impossible to bring them together within anything more than a formal unity, but on its own each of these dominant directions offers very little for developing the phenomenological basis of the analysis being initiated here.

The difficulty now becomes greater insofar as definite phenomenal characteristics need to be made visible and brought into relief within this being-interpreted in the today. The necessary basis for this analysis is present neither where finished philosophical systems are already at hand nor where interest is focused on plans for such a system. We will not be discussing propositions in their finished form, results, so as to ask about their truth or falsity. It would be better if for the time being the assumption were made that everything said in today's philosophy is pure and incontrovertible truth. In the analysis, our looking will be directed rather to what goes on in philosophy before it becomes what it is. Not even a methodology or logic of philosophy could give a proper explanation of this, because it would itself have to be a theory in the same sense as this philosophy itself.

What the analysis asks for is simply the opportunity to reactivate step by step the kind of investigation and the context of its actualization which have led to the system and its absolute truths, and to do this in order to get a grasp of the manner in which propositions are demonstrated and proven in relation to their thematic object, i.e., to bring into relief here how the object stands in view and is being looked at, how it is being interrogated, how concepts are being drawn from it. Hence a quite primitive kind of request. (Mind you, today's distinguished philosophers either consider such questions to be nothing more than unmannerly intrusiveness or else they cannot even understand how it makes sense to ask about such a thing.)

Every attempt to supply such a basis for the analysis comes up blank. The only remaining possibility is to proceed with a characterization of the main traits of the comportment of knowing which can be drawn out of the systems and their basic tendency. This comporting was already defined as universal classifying, one which is carried out by classifying temporality in terms of the eternal and, as it were, filing it away into it.

This *classifying and filing away of something into something* takes its point of departure from the temporal itself, within the concrete. With this in mind, today's philosophers believe themselves to be proceeding far better than Hegel, though Hegel had a more concrete notion of the concrete matters of which he spoke than all the philosophers after him who construct systems.

One takes one's point of departure within the concrete, within nature and culture or rather only within culture since even though nature becomes an object only in the natural sciences, these sciences are themselves cultural goods, ones belonging to the cultural system called "science." (Earlier one said: *nature is spirit.*)

As universal classification, philosophy encompasses the totality of culture, it is the system of cultural systems. But this totality is not itself examined as a theme in philosophy. The temporal is not itself investigated, but rather is that *from out of which* the classifying takes its point of departure, the point of departure for defining it in such a manner that it is inserted into a context of classification.

And this means: the comporting at the point of departure of classifying runs through the temporal in such a manner that it grasps it in advance in terms of its *types*, its essential generalities. Only when the concrete has been defined in advance in *such* a manner does it have the conceptual makeup as an object which is necessary for it to be able to enter in any manner into a context of classification.

This "typifying" comportment at the point of departure "uses" the "empirical material" provided by the sciences of culture—it takes up what has already been made available (in a readymade characterization) in the comportment of that curiosity which is pulled along by its objects. However, the work of classifying does not tarry there, but only begins there, i.e., it moves on.

The real interests of the comportment of knowing do not allow it to remain at this transitional stage. The unmistakable documentation of this is the fact that the immanent character of the method of this comporting at the point of departure, i.e., the one which is relevant for its actualizing, remains conspicuously undefined in philosophy. (The only concrete investigation of this: Husserl, *Logical Investigations,* Vol. II/1, 2nd Investigation[1]—and this itself stays within a very specific domain of objects, those defined by thinghood.)

How little everyone is disturbed about this is shown by how that from which they take their point of departure is characterized as an object: the temporal and empirical, the mutable, subjective, real, and singular, the individual and contingent in contrast to the trans-temporal and trans-empirical (the a priori), the immutable, objective, trans-temporal, ideal, universal, and necessary. Categorial definitions from the *most disparate sources* are in each case haphazardly employed to characterize the basis from out of which the classifying begins to run it course. That the comporting at the point of departure is unworried about its own concrete and precise clarification when the classifying and filing away is being

---

1. 2d rev. ed. (Halle, 1913), pp. 106-224. [*Logical Investigations,* Vol. 1, trans. J. N. Findlay (London: Routledge & Kegan Paul, 1970), pp. 337-432.]

done (the conceptual definitions remain at the level at which Plato left them) is only a symptom of the fact that its objects are "only" material for a typology and system of classification.

The idea of knowledge striven after here is thereby already sketched out in advance. The basic tendency of the comporting is classifying and filing away into . . . , i.e., something concrete is considered to be known when one has defined *where* it belongs, the place within the totality of the classificatory order *whereinto* it is to be inserted—something is seen to be defined when it has been put away.

Here it is a difference of a secondary order whether this classifying and accommodating in the totality actualizes itself in the manner of a filing away into an already finished and static system, be it closed or open, or whether the total classificatory order is precisely something which first develops in and through the typifying and classifying and first comes into its proper being in this self-development. The accommodating of the typified concrete objects in the total classificatory order is then not an allocation of places in a readymade framework, but rather a marking out of stations in the process of the system itself.

Having the character of process, this mobile system is of course something "more profound" than the static and more objective kind of system. In fact, the character of the actualizing of the comportment of knowing comes to light all the more clearly in the system defined by process. As a universal system, the "whereinto" of the classifying must itself be set in motion and held in motion—if observation were to come to a standstill at a certain station of the process, this would indeed be tantamount to naive "empirical knowledge," a sin against the H. Spirit of knowledge itself!

The following three self-motivating and self-conditioning modes of comporting have become relatively clear in the context of the actualization of the universal classifying of philosophy: (1) the comporting at the point of departure—the running through of the totality of cultural objects which collects and typifies them, i.e., makes them available as material; (2) the accommodating of the multiplicity of types in a total classificatory order which allocates places for them and puts them away there; (3) the *developing* of the *context of the classificatory order* itself which provides these places. This third mode is the leading one (in a manner analogous to historical consciousness: the holding-in-view of style), putting the first two into its service and thus giving them a real tendency.

The third mode is not the mere depicting of something, but rather a creative developing of the classificatory order itself—it fashions from out of itself and for itself the possibility of a *universal process*. Its result is the universal running through of the intrinsically interlocking, absolute context of relations of the classificatory order which is valid in itself. The relational definitions of the classificatory order are not juxtapositions in the manner of "the one *and* then the other *and* then the next and so on," but rather the one is defined as that which belongs to the other. It is in itself it itself as well as the other, i.e., *all* others. (What forehaving? that of looking away!) The *as-well-as* provides, and indeed does so in the limitlessness of its universality, the fundamental formal and categorial structure of the context of objects of the absolute classificatory order.

Its development, i.e., the appropriate comportment of system-building and holding ourselves in this comportment, consists in the universal being-in-motion of the defining, in the fundamental *being-everywhere-and-nowhere* of the comportment of knowing. And indeed this being-everywhere-and-nowhere is quite distinctive, i.e., it does not merely abandon itself to a pregiven realm of objects, letting itself be pulled along by them simply as they happen to be encountered, but rather it is a knowing and defining which, in developing the process of the classificatory order, is constantly developing its own possibility, of itself directing itself to the possibility of being in constant and universal movement. So long as the context of the classificatory order is such that there is a standstill somewhere in it, it has not been perfected, i.e., has not come into its own and its innermost possibility.

This being-everywhere-and-nowhere of philosophical knowing is not curiosity which is simply pulled along by its object. Rather, free-standing and ushering itself into its own possibility, it is in a broader sense an *absolute curiosity which leads itself along.*

As a mode of interpretation, even philosophy is in the open space of publicness—it *is* there in the mode of everything public, i.e., it makes itself present and puts itself forward in the public realm, making itself a topic of discussion, so as to contribute to the general talk, give itself a foothold in life, and preserve itself in it. The self-interpretation of this autonomous curiosity is stating publicly what it thinks it is all about and comes to, and it is doing this precisely in its free-standing manner.

At the same time, its self-interpretation is public not in the sense that it is merely putting into "circulation" a knowledge of the features with which it is outfitted, but rather in the sense that it is making a demand, one which is imposed on Dasein itself and which it is supposed to go along with. The self-interpretation of curiosity publicly holds up before this curiosity its tasks and, after the fashion of all publicness, pushes it straight into them, i.e., in its self-interpretation this free-standing curiosity helps itself to still more of what it already is, facilitates curiosity in such a manner that it can procure fresh "food for thought" from Dasein itself.

In its self-interpretation, philosophical consciousness concretely puts itself forward in the public domain of educational interests from the following four points of view:

1. as the *objective* scientific kind of philosophy. In it "absolute truths" free of standpoints are brought to light, and the uncritical arbitrariness

of worldview-philosophy and its contingent pictures of life are neutralized. Having the thematic definition and mode of treatment described above, philosophy is the proper refuge in which Dasein is protected from an abysmal *relativism*.

2. As this objective kind of philosophy, it offers Dasein itself the view of reality which it has coming to it and in which alone it can possibly find a secure hold for itself. It is not only not mere worldview-philosophy, but offers every possible worldview the opportunity of being oriented to fundamental points of reference and reinforced with them. Amid the snarl of worldviews putting forth their opinions and conducting their experiments, it brings the objective possibility of a more objective *agreement*, the "All of us . . . ," i.e., it makes present and offers to Dasein itself the prospect of the tranquil certainty and security of the general and unanimous "yes, I agree" in contrast to the unproductive work of fragmentation in the rampant *skepticism* of our day, which is, as Rickert says, merely an affair for "philosophical weaklings."

3. Moreover, in offering genuine certainty and security, this objective scientific kind of philosophy is so little a mere academic pursuit which runs away from life and abandons itself to a transcendence located "beyond" life that "life itself" is rather, so to speak, captured in it. As something dynamic, the system itself has precisely the character of process of *life itself,* i.e., this philosophy alone has what "everyone" today really demands of it for their Dasein—what is called being "true to life."

4. As the kind of philosophy which is true to life, but without being for that "merely" subjective, it is simultaneously *universal* and *concrete,* i.e., what it has to offer is precisely what there is a general need for: getting away from *specialization* and shortsighted trivial perspectives on problems.

By way of summary: philosophy offers Dasein an objective refuge, the prospect of the tranquillizing certainty and security of agreement, the splendor of the immediacy of being true to life, and indeed, in unison with this, overcoming the shortwinded, overly detailed kind of inquiry which slowly inches along and shies away from grand solutions.

Absolute "freedom from needs" (Hegel)[2] is achieved. "Spirit" now lives in the abode of its self-certainty. We no longer give ourselves over to feelings, goals, interests. Life has retired into its authentic freedom.

§13. Further tasks of hermeneutics

What already showed itself in the modes of comporting of each of the two above-mentioned directions of interpretation (historical conscious-

2. *Wissenschaft der Logik, 1. Teil,* p. 12. [*Hegel's Science of Logic,* p. 34 (modified).]

ness and philosophy) has now pushed to the fore all the more tangibly in their self-interpretations. What needs to be seen in our interpretive assessment is that, in both of these modes of the interpretation of Dasein, Dasein itself is out for and going toward something, i.e., *having itself objectively there for itself,* bringing itself *objectively* into its there. The basic phenomenon of *curiosity* which lives and is at work in these two modes of interpretation, being pulled along by its object in the one and leading itself along in a free-standing manner in the other, shows Dasein in its peculiar kind of *movement.*

And this means that historical consciousness, "history," and philosophy are at bottom not mere cultural goods which lie around in books, provide a source of occasional amusement, or offer a possible employment and livelihood, but rather they are modes *of the being-there of Dasein,* paths[46] which are held open and preserved in it itself, on which *it is under way* and *finds itself* in its characteristic manner (of falling away), i.e., on which it *is taking possession of itself,* i.e., *making itself certain and secure* about itself.

What was decisive here: the certainty is objective certainty. In both modes of interpretation, Dasein is encountering itself exactly as it is in itself, free of standpoints. Historical consciousness lets Dasein be encountered in the entire wealth of the objective being of its *having-been,* while philosophy lets it be encountered in the immutability of its *always-being-in-such-a-manner.* Both directions of interpretation bring Dasein itself before its highest and pure *present.* A temporal definition is at play in these objective descriptions. We need to explain why.

Our task is to bring factical Dasein into view, have a look at it, and gain an understanding of the character of its being. Accordingly, the *further course of the hermeneutical analysis* is already sketched out in advance. The basic phenomenon of *curiosity* needs to be uncovered categorially

1. as a *movement* of Dasein itself, i.e., what needs to be explained, brought into relief in an analysis employing intuition for its demonstrations, is in what sense Dasein is movement and this movement a how of temporality, of facticity. The meaning of this word needs to be drawn from a fund of subject matters which have to be seen in a primordial manner.

2. And curiosity as a movement in such a manner that the Dasein which "is" this movement "has" itself there in it—thus a fundamental categorial structure of the phenomenon of the *being*-there of Dasein [*Da*-seins] in the how of its *having*-itself-there, a phenomenon to be uncovered by an ontology of life. The ontological structure of the phenomenon of being-interpreted will thereby become visible at the same time, i.e., it will now become possible to demonstrate phenomenally what we stated at the start simply in the form of a thesis—the characteristics of being-interpreted can now be unveiled as categories of Dasein as such, i.e., as existentials.

3. In connection with this stands the task of clarifying the *fundamental phenomenon of the "there"* and providing a categorial-ontological characterization of Dasein's *being*-there, of its *being*-this-there.[47] It is in the presence of the existentials showing up in this analysis that we need to see Dasein, and in seeing and understanding it,

4. we need to go back to our point of departure and hermeneutically pose the question: *as what*, then, is Dasein there for itself in the above-mentioned modes of interpretation, and what characteristic of its being is found in this mode of being-there-in-such-a-manner?

What then needs to be decided is whether philosophy and history — just as they offer themselves to life in their self-interpretations — have grasped Dasein, or whether they are as such not rather possibilities running counter to it?

The analysis will begin by engaging itself in the task mentioned under 2. and will indeed do this by choosing a very primitive point of departure in which the above-mentioned phenomena of Dasein, the two modes of interpretation, are not initially visible. (See the insert for p. 14 [of the manuscript].)[1]

---

1. This "insert" is missing from H.'s manuscript of the course. A student transcript has been used in its place. See Editor's Epilogue.

PART TWO

THE PHENOMENOLOGICAL PATH OF
THE HERMENEUTICS OF FACTICITY

Chapter One

Preliminary Reflections: Phenomenon and Phenomenology

But some preliminary reflections must be taken care of first. The expression "phenomenon" or "phenomenal" has already been used various times and indeed with special emphasis. These terms and, correspondingly, "phenomenology" need to be discussed only to the extent that this can serve as a guide regarding method. Moreover: talking *about* phenomenology is inconsequential. Any explanation of this kind is not simply a matter of supplying a word with an already established meaning, but rather if it understands what it needs to do, it will necessarily be an interpretation of the history of the meaning of the term in question. Such an interpretation can be given here only in a summary form which will allow us to gain an initial understanding.

§14. On the history of "phenomenology"

The word "phenomenon" has its origin in the Greek term φαινόμενον which derives from φαίνεσθαι, showing itself. A phenomenon is thus that which shows itself as something showing itself. This means that it is itself there and is not merely represented in some manner, examined indirectly, or somehow reconstructed. "Phenomenon" is a mode of being-an-object and indeed a distinctive one: being-present as an object from out of itself. This initially says nothing at all about the content of the subject matter, it gives no directive to a definite domain of subject matter. "Phenomenon" means a distinctive mode of being-an-object.

When the term is used in this manner, what is also involved is a rejection of certain modes of being-an-object which are not genuine, but are still possible for beings and indeed factically dominant.

It is in this sense that the term became influential in the *history of science* and indeed eventually in the natural sciences of the nineteenth century. Here a self-interpretation regarding their basic tendency made itself known. As sciences of physical phenomena, they define these beings just as they show themselves in experience, a definite mode of access to them, and they define them only to the extent that they show themselves. They do not speculate about invisible properties and hidden powers (*qualitates occultae* [occult qualities]).

They thereby represented and put forward the self-interpretation of all scientific disciplines in the nineteenth century. It was to them that the human sciences and philosophy oriented themselves. The work of philosophy concentrated more and more on theory of science, logic in the broadest sense. And, in addition to logic, on psychology—both of these took their *orientation from the natural sciences,* and indeed epistemology did this in such a manner that it saw genuine knowledge to be realized in the natural sciences. It searched for the conditions of such knowledge which can be found in consciousness. Purportedly in the spirit of Kant and yet claiming to go beyond him, one attempted to do the same for the human sciences. Here one saw the main business at hand to be that of demarcation—and here the natural sciences were the standard *per negationem* [via negation].

In formulating his theory of the human sciences as a "critique of historical reason,"[1] even Dilthey, who originally came out of history and theology, conspicuously relied on this Kantian approach.

Rickert and Windelband are only scions of what Dilthey tackled in concrete research and indeed with far scantier resources. Only today is one beginning to notice that the problem of the human sciences needs to be tackled with very different conceptual resources.

Psychology adopted even the method of the natural sciences and sought to build factical life up from ultimate elements—impressions. (Today's psychology sees its object differently, not least of all due to the influence of phenomenology.)

In contrast to the misunderstandings which occurred in this imitation of the natural sciences, Brentano in his *Psychology from an Empirical Standpoint* cleared a path for imitating them in a *genuine* manner. Analogous to what had been done in the natural sciences, he posed the task of investigating psychical phenomena. As in the natural sciences, the theory being put forward is supposed to be drawn from the things themselves. The classification of psychical beings, i.e., of the various modes of experiencing, is not supposed to be initiated from on high in a constructivistic manner, i.e., precisely *not* with the categories of the natural sciences. It must rather be obtained from a study of the things themselves, from how they show themselves.

In the last decades of the nineteenth century, the work of philosophy

---

1. See *Einleitung in die Geisteswissenschaften. Versuch einer Grundlegung für das Studium der Gesellschaft und der Geschichte* (Leipzig, 1883), p. 145; 4th ed. in *Gesammelte Schriften*, Vol. 1 (Stuttgart and Göttingen, 1959), p. 116. [*Introduction to the Human Sciences: An Attempt to Lay a Foundation for the Study of Society and History*, trans. R. Betanzos (Detroit: Wayne State University, 1988), p. 146.]

was thus applied mainly to the phenomenon of consciousness. This is why the claim surfaced in psychology that, as the true science of consciousness, it provides the premise of epistemology and logic. Here the phenomena of consciousness appear as experiences and their unifying context as life. But the starting point still remained the same. Fundamental reflections on the object of philosophy did not occur—nonetheless, the tendency of philosophy of life must be approached in a positive sense as a breakthrough to a more radical tendency of philosophizing, even though its foundations are inadequate.

It was out of this intellectual situation that Husserl's *Logical Investigations* arose. They are investigations of objects which traditionally belong in the domain of logic. The kind of investigation involved was characterized as phenomenology, i.e., descriptive psychology. The mode of questioning was: where are the objects about which logic speaks and how are they there for it? If what logic says is to have a solid basis, then it is necessary that these things become accessible as they are in themselves. Concepts and propositions about concepts and propositions must be drawn from the objects themselves, e.g., propositions are encountered as written or spoken assertions which are read or heard. Assertions which are guided by experiences of thought and knowledge and the latter in turn by experiences of meaning. What is found in assertions is both their *about-which* and *what* they assert, two things which do not coincide with "subject" and "object." Thus everything depends upon our grasp of such experiences, upon our grasping that consciousness is consciousness of something. This was the primitive task.

Husserl was influenced here by the work of Brentano, and this was the case not only regarding his method in that he adopted Brentano's method of description, but also regarding his basic definition of the domain of experience as his subject matter. Brentano had characterized consciousness of something as *intentionality*. This concept arose in the Middle Ages and had at that time a narrower sphere of application, it meant a volitional being-out-for-something and going-toward-it (ὄρεξις [desire]).

In a fundamental critique of his teacher, Husserl now took a fundamental step beyond him, explaining the phenomenon Brentano had indicated with the term "intentionality" in such a manner that he provided more firmly established guidelines for research into experiences and contexts of experience. His critique was one in which he followed up on and radicalized the tendencies which were at work in Brentano's approach, but had still not yet arrived at a real breakthrough.

But Husserl's *Logical Investigations* were not really understood and perhaps to this day still are not. Epistemology still does not understand that all theories of judgment are basically theories of presentation (cf. H. Rickert, *The Object of Knowledge*—its foundations are utterly dilettantish[2]). Regarding what its object was, nothing had changed in Husserl's *Logical Investigations*. Rather, what was drummed into the philosophical consciousness of that time was simply *the question of access*. The subject matter remained the same—the only thing different was the *how* of interrogating and defining it, i.e., description versus a constructivistic and deductive method. And this how of investigation not merely as an idle prospect and program, but rather it was something concretely initiated and the reader was shown how to do it.

"Phenomenon" is thus not primarily a category, but initially has to do with the how of access, of grasping and bringing into true safekeeping.[48] Phenomenology is therefore initially nothing other than a *mode of research*, namely: addressing something just as it shows itself and only to the extent that it shows itself. Hence an utter triviality for any scientific discipline, and yet since Aristotle it has slipped further and further out of the grasp of philosophy.

Another point needs to be added: For Husserl, a definite ideal of science was prescribed in *mathematics* and the mathematical natural sciences. Mathematics was the model for all scientific disciplines. This scientific ideal came into play in that one attempted to elevate description to the level of mathematical rigor.

Nothing more needs to be said here about this absolutizing of mathematical rigor. This is not the first time it has surfaced, but rather it has for a long time dominated science, finding an apparent justification in the general idea of science which appeared among the Greeks, where one believed that knowledge was to be found in knowledge of universals and—what is seen to be the same thing—knowledge of what is universally valid. But this is all a mistake. And when one cannot attain such mathematical rigor, one gives up.

Fundamentally, one does not even realize that a prejudice is at work here. Is it justified to hold up mathematics as a model for all scientific disciplines? Or are the basic relations between mathematics and the other disciplines not thereby stood on their heads? Mathematics is the least rigorous of disciplines, because it is the one easiest to gain access to. The human sciences presuppose much more scientific existence than could ever be achieved by a mathematician. One should approach a scientific discipline not as a system of propositions and grounds for justifying them, but rather as something in which factical Dasein critically confronts itself and explicates itself. To bring mathematics into play as the model for all scientific disciplines is unphenomenological—the meaning of scientific

---

2. *Der Gegenstand der Erkenntnis. Einführung in die Transzendentalphilosophie*, 3d entirely rev. and expanded ed. (Tübingen, 1915).

rigor needs rather to be drawn from the kind of object being investigated and the mode of access appropriate to it.

Phenomenology is thus a *how of research* which makes the objects in question present in intuition and discusses them only to the extent that they are there in such intuition. This how and its execution are self-evident. This is why it is at bottom misleading to say "phenomenological philosophy." This would be the same as an art historian also wanting to emphasize explicitly that what he does is scientific history of art. But this expression does have a certain propaedeutic legitimacy, given that its self-evidence has slipped out of our grasp. This self-evidence thus does not constitute a new school of philosophy. This how of research was at first applied to the objects of logic—the "what" and the "about-which" remained traditional.

Thus did phenomenology make its first beginning. On the basis of this situation, the meaning of the thematic category of "phenomenon" had to be reworked into a *regional* category. Thus it encompassed those objects characterized with the terms "experiences" and "contexts of consciousness." Here experiences as experiences are the phenomena. Thus one domain of being was demarcated over against others. Phenomena were now the objects of a specific science.

The further development of phenomenology is characterized by four moments:

1. The thematic domain which had been designated with the term "consciousness" and thereby included the totality of the real and intentional content of the stream of experience was held fast. The horizon for posing questions about it and the basic approach to it came in from elsewhere: what came from the Marburg school was the posing of epistemological questions (characteristic of both is a return to Descartes), and Dilthey was consulted on the issue of laying the foundation of the human sciences (nature and mind).

   Thus transcendental idealism entered into phenomenology. And the countermovement to this also arose in phenomenology by taking up traditional realism. These opposites became the guiding foci for academic discussions within the different directions phenomenology took. No one raised the radical question of whether epistemological questions might not in fact be meaningless in phenomenology. Everyone went to work within a bad tradition.

2. The investigations carried out in the field of logic were also applied to other traditional domains of inquiry. In line with the approach and the kind of person doing the work, a specific model of inquiry was in each case picked up from the tradition. One set to work with a limited fund of phenomenological distinctions.

3. The drive for a system is noticeable everywhere—what we said earlier about the philosophical consciousness of today also holds here.

4. What has resulted from the escalation of these three moments and from the infiltration of traditional terminology into phenomenology is a general watering down. Everyone acknowledges the affinity between the opposing sides. Phenomenological research, which was supposed to provide a basis for scientific work, has sunk to the level of wishy-washiness, thoughtlessness, and summariness, to the level of the philosophical noise of the day, to the level of a public scandal of philosophy. The industry surrounding schools and their students has blocked the avenues of access for actually taking up phenomenology and doing it. The George circle, Keyserling, anthroposophy, Steiner, etc.—everything absorbs phenomenology. How far it has gone is shown by a recent book, *Phenomenology of Mysticism*, which appeared with an authorized publisher and with the most official sponsorship.[3] Beware of all this!

This is the way matters stand in lieu of one taking up phenomenology as a possibility. It is impossible to make out anything about phenomenology or obtain a definition of it from this philosophical industry. The business is hopeless! All such tendencies are a betrayal of phenomenology and its possibilities. The ruin can no longer be halted!

§15. Phenomenology in accord with its possibility as a how of research

Phenomenology needs to be understood *in accord with its possibility* as something which is not publicly and self-evidently given. Any *possibility has its proper mode of being taken up and brought into true safekeeping*, it is not simply to be picked up as a theme and treated in a businesslike fashion—taking up a possibility means rather: taking it up in its being and developing it, i.e., what is sketched out in advance in it regarding possibilities.

Phenomenology is thus a distinctive *how of research*. Objects come to be defined just as they give themselves. What investigation is required to hold to is the task of presenting the subject matter in question. Here we can lay out in advance a path which the hermeneutics of facticity attempts to travel.

Objects are to be taken just as they show themselves in themselves, i.e., just as they are encountered by a *definite manner of looking toward them and seeing them*. This seeing arises out of and on the basis of a being-oriented

---

3. G. Walther, *Zur Phänomenologie der Mystik* (place of publication not given, 1923; Olten and Freiburg, 3d ed., 1976).

regarding the objects, an already-being-familiar with these beings. Being-familiar with them is for the most part the sedimented result of having heard about them and having learned something about them. The about-which is here present in a traditional interpretation or characterization, e.g., logic in a definite manner of classifying it, characterizing it, and seeing its problems.

The situation of a discipline at any particular time [*jeweilige Lage*] is such that it stands face to face with the definite manner in which the things it studies stand at that moment. Their showing-themselves can be an aspect which has become so restricted and fixed through *tradition* that this inauthenticity is no longer able to be recognized, but rather is taken to be what is authentic, the actual things in question. What shows itself from itself in a straightforward manner need not as yet be the subject matter itself. Insofar as one leaves it at that, one has already in establishing a foundation passed off a contingency as an in-itself. One takes a covering up of the subject matter for the subject matter itself.

Hence taking up the subject matter in a straightforward manner guarantees nothing at all. What is needed is to get beyond the position started from and arrive at a grasp of the subject matter which is free of covering up. For this it is necessary to disclose the history of the covering up of the subject matter. The tradition of philosophical questioning must be pursued all the way back to the original sources of its subject matter. The tradition must be dismantled. Only in this way is a primordial position on the subject matter possible. This regress places philosophy once again before the decisive contexts.

Such is possible today only through fundamental *historical critique*. This is not a mere exercise in providing convenient historical illustrations, but rather a fundamental task of philosophy itself. How convenient everyone makes it for themselves is shown by the absence of history in phenomenology: one naively believes that the subject matter will, no matter what the position of looking at it, be obtained in *plain and simple evidence*. Also characteristic is the dilettantism with which opinions are picked up from history and reworked. One turns history into a story.

The dismantling takes its point of departure from a presentation of today's situation—and if philosophical research here looks to be something quite protracted, then one will just have to accept that, find one's way around in it, and wait. Not every time needs to have a grand philosophical system.

When the tradition is critically dismantled, the possibility of getting bogged down in seemingly important problems no longer remains. Dismantling, here this means: a regress to Greek philosophy, to Aristotle, in order to see how a certain original dimension came to be fallen away from and covered up and to see that we are situated in this *falling away*. The original position needs to be redeveloped in a manner appropriate to our position, i.e., in a manner appropriate to the changed historical situation, it becomes something different and yet remains the same.

What is thereby given for the first time is the possibility of hitting upon the object of philosophy in a primordial manner and striking out into it. The concrete tendency of demonstration must bring itself into play and do its fundamental work by providing and sketching out in advance the character of being of the object of philosophy, as well as the character of the way in which it becomes an object for us and of the right way to gain access to it and bring it into true safekeeping.

In this matter, philosophy today still moves within the tradition. As a thematic category for the stance of accessing the object and the preparedness for dealing with it, *"phenomenon"* means a constant *preparation of the path to be traveled*. This thematic category has the function of a critical cautionary guidance of seeing in a regress along a path of dismantling critically detected instances of covering up. It is a critical reminder, i.e., to be understood only in its function of cautioning us and is misunderstood if taken as a demarcation. (Individual sciences are demarcated by those who are at home in them and practice them. When philosophy interferes with this, that is quackery.)

Should it turn out that *to be in* the mode of *covering-itself-up* and self-veiling belongs to the character of *being of the being* [Seinscharakter des Seins] which constitutes the object of philosophy, and indeed not in an accessorial sense but in accord with the character of its being, then the category of "phenomenon" will become a truly earnest matter. The task involved — making it a phenomenon — will become phenomenological in a radical sense.

This is the path the *hermeneutics of facticity* attempts to travel. It calls itself interpretation, i.e., it does not merely depict matters in terms of the aspect under which they first appear. All interpreting is an interpreting with respect to something, on the basis of it, and with a view to it. The *forehaving*, which is to be interpretively explicated, must be put into the context of the object and seen there.[49] One must step away from the subject matter initially given and back to that on which it is based. The progress of hermeneutics must arise out of looking at its object itself. Decisive factors have been provided by Husserl. But here it is necessary to be able to heed and to learn. Instead, one finds an industry generated from ignorance of subject matter.

Chapter Two

"The Being-There of Dasein Is Being in a World"[1]

§16. The formal indication of a forehaving

What was said about "phenomenon" and "phenomenology" has nothing to do with providing a methodology for phenomenology, an undertaking of the most dubious kind—it simply has the function of an orienting which has illuminated a certain stretch of the path of inquiry, of a pause within a certain traveling and seeing along this path. What was said is intended to be understood solely in this respect and with a view to it. By way of the most necessary considerations of method, we will shortly make the explicit passage from understanding the how of research in an empty manner to actually taking it up.

Through a first examination of the being-there of Dasein in its today, where the position of our looking was focused on the phenomenon of "being-interpreted," two directions of interpretation were brought into relief in this Dasein. They showed themselves as modes in which Dasein is speaking to itself and about itself in a pronounced manner, i.e., in which it makes itself present for itself, holds itself in this presence, and lingers in it. As so characterized, Dasein's having-itself-there sees itself in historical consciousness in the kind of being which consists in a certain having-been of itself, and in philosophy in the kind of the being which consists in a certain always-being-in-such-a-manner. In both directions of interpretation, i.e., in the basic phenomenon of being-interpreted, the phenomenon of *curiosity* showed itself and indeed it did so as the how of a self-comporting (of being) which consists in being-directed toward something in the mode of knowing and defining it.

What is necessary is to bring this phenomenon authentically into view in intuition and indeed in such a way that Dasein itself, in accord with the basic tendency to hermeneutical investigation in it, discloses itself with regard to definite characteristics of its being. Accordingly, Dasein itself must be able to be looked at within the thematic field of our inquiry in a more explicit manner than previously.

The possibility and productivity of a concrete explication of the phenomenon of curiosity is (like that of any phenomenon) rooted in *what* Dasein is in advance approached and defined *as* in its basic traits. Looking toward something and seeing it and the defining of what-is-held-in-sight

---

1. From this point onward, the text is again based on H.'s manuscript.

(a defining which works within the looking-toward and actualizes it in the sense of developing it) already in advance "have" what they wish to look into as such and such a being—what is had in advance in this manner and is found in each instance of accessing and dealing with the matter in question can be designated as a *forehaving*.

The fate of our approach to phenomena and our execution of concrete hermeneutical descriptions of them hangs on the level of the primordiality and genuineness of the forehaving into which Dasein as such (factical life) has been placed.

The forehaving in which Dasein (in each case our own Dasein in its being-there for a while at the particular time)[50] stands for this investigation can be expressed in a formal indication: *the being-there of Dasein (factical life) is being in a world*. This forehaving should already find its demonstration precisely in our analysis of curiosity. If such a demonstration is successful, then this still does not say anything about the primordiality of the forehaving—it is itself only a phenomenon of another forehaving which lies further back right within it and has already been at work in our descriptions.

The forehaving needs to be more closely examined and appropriated so that the empty intelligibility of the above formal indication can be filled out by looking in the direction of its concrete source in intuition. A *formal indication* is always misunderstood when it is treated as a fixed universal proposition and used to make deductions from and fantasized with in a constructivistic dialectical fashion. Everything depends upon our understanding being guided from out of the indefinite and vague but still intelligible content of the indication onto the right *path of looking*. Successfully getting onto this path can and must be aided by a precautionary measure which takes the form of rejecting certain positions of looking which are dominant in the situation of research at the particular time [*jeweiligen Lage*], which *seem* relevant, and which thus of themselves crowd in upon us.

§17. Misunderstandings

A. The subject-object schema

This *schema* must be avoided: *What exists are subjects and objects*, consciousness and being—being is the object of knowledge—being in the authentic sense is the being of nature—consciousness is an "I think," thus an ego, ego-pole, center of acts, person—egos (persons) have standing opposite them: beings, objects, natural things, things of value, goods. The relation between subject and object needs to be explained and is a problem for epistemology.

This problem forms the basis of all those possibilities which are tried out over and over again and let loose on each other in endless discussions: the object is dependent on the subject, or the subject on the object, or both on each other in a correlative manner. This constructivistic forehaving, almost ineradicable on account of the pertinacity of a sedimented tradition, fundamentally and forever obstructs access to that which we have indicated with the term "factical life" ("Dasein"). No modification of this schema would be able to do away with its inappropriateness. The schema itself has developed historically within the tradition from different constructions of each of its components (subject and object) which proceeded in isolation from one another and were then integrated in various ways.

The disastrous infiltration of this schema into phenomenological research was already underscored in the description of the historical situation out of which phenomenology arose. The dominance of this epistemological problem (and corresponding ones in other disciplines) is characteristic of a widely observed kind of activity through which academic disciplines, especially philosophy, gain a foothold in life and preserve themselves. 90% of the literature is preoccupied with ensuring that such wrongheaded problems not disappear and are confounded still more and in ever new ways. Such literature dominates the industry—everyone sees and gauges the progress and vitality of academic disciplines with it.

Unnoticed in the midst of all this are those who quietly put a stranglehold on such pseudo-problems (Husserl's *Logical Investigations*!) and see to it for those who have understood something of all this that they no longer investigate such things. Such negative influences are the most decisive ones and for just this reason impervious to all chatter in the public realm.

B. The prejudice of freedom from standpoints

Rejecting this way of proceeding in which the subject-object schema is foisted on fields of investigation is only one of the most urgent precautionary measures needed today. A second concerns a prejudice which merely constitutes the counterpart to the uncritical approach of generating constructions and theorizing. This is the *demand for observation which is free of standpoints.*

This second prejudice is even more disastrous for research because, with its express watchword for the seemingly highest idea of science and objectivity, it in fact elevates taking an uncritical approach into a first principle and promulgates a fundamental blindness. It cultivates a strange modesty and grants a general dispensation from critical questioning by means of the apparent self-evidence of what it demands. For what could be more obvious even to the slowest than the demand for an unbiased approach to the subject matter—and thus for suspending one's stand-point? (The motives behind this idea of freedom from standpoints?)

(Free of standpoints only when there is nothing to be done, but what if we actually have to look at matters and carry out research on them? A free-standing detached standpoint = the ruin of being-a-subject. De-veloping our standpoint is prior on the level of being. The right way of doing this which we must be capable of recognizing prejudices and indeed regarding not just their content but also their being. Public tol-erance—as against *that,* the prior genuine way of entering the world, lifting the controls on it, giving it free play.[51])

Even unbiased seeing is a seeing and as such has its position of looking and indeed has it in a distinctive manner, i.e., by having explicitly appropriated it so that it has been critically purged.

If the term is to say anything at all, *"freedom from standpoints"* is nothing other than an explicit *appropriation of our position of looking.* This position is itself something historical, i.e., bound up with Dasein (re-sponsibility, how Dasein stands regarding itself), and not a chimerical in-itself outside of time.

Chapter Three

The Development of the Forehaving

§18. A look at everydayness

With these two prejudicial positions of looking having been rejected as a precautionary measure, the above-mentioned forehaving itself and the path of looking with respect to, on the basis of, and with a view to it now need to be made visible and actualized. The being-there of Dasein is what it is in the awhileness of temporal particularity, but its being-there in this awhileness needs itself to be placed under very different points of view.

What is decisive for the development of a forehaving is seeing Dasein in its *everydayness*. Everydayness is a characteristic of the temporality of Dasein (foreconception). What belongs to everydayness is a certain averageness of Dasein, the *"every-one,"* in which the fact that Dasein is "our own" and the possibility of authenticity keep themselves covered up.

It is in this tendency of looking toward Dasein in its being-there for a while at the particular time[52] *in average everydayness* that the formal indication of the forehaving, "factical life (the being-there of Dasein) means being in a world," is to be demonstrated in intuition. What is meant by *"world"*? What does *"in"* a world mean? And what does *"being"* in a world look like? We will not be piecing together the phenomenon of the being-there of Dasein out of these different definitions, but rather our focus at the particular time [*jeweiligen Betonung*] on a *single* term in this formal indication will always be but one possible point of view on the same unitary phenomenon.

(What does "world" as the "wherein" of being mean? The answer will run through the following *stations* of intuitive presentation: The world is something being encountered.[53] As what and how is it being encountered? Encountering it and the character of its being (an "object" only for formal ontology). In the character of references (a technical term, ontological) — references give the world as something we are concerned about and attend to — it is "there" in the how of being-of-concern. The immediate character of the there and being-encountered of its being-of-concern. As something we are concerned about and attend to, the world is there as an environing world, environs, the round-about.[54]

What we are concerned about and attend to shows itself as that *wherefrom, out of which,* and *on the basis of which* factical life is lived. Explicated in such a manner, this wherefrom, out-of-which, and on-the-basis-of-which will provide the phenomenological basis for understanding being *"in"* a world,[55] i.e., for a primordial interpretation of the phenomenon of factical spatiality turning up there and the phenomenon of being *"in"* it. The how of this being-*"in"* [*"in"-Sein*] as a living *from out of* the world as what is being encountered in concern shows itself as caring.)[1]

What does the world as the "wherein" of being mean? The answer will run through the following *stations of intuitive presentation:* The world is something being encountered. The as-what and how of its being-encountered lie in what will be designated as *significance.* Significance is not a category of things, one which gathers together into a separate domain certain objects with content in contrast to other kinds of objects and demarcates them over against another region of objects. It is rather a how of being, and indeed the categorial dimension of the being-there[56] of the world is centered in it. The being of the world and that of human life are designated in the same manner with the term "being-there" — why this is so will soon become clear.

This world is something being encountered as *what we are concerned about and attend to,* and the latter, as having the character of initial givens now and soon to come which are closest to us, gives to the world of everydayness the character of an *environing world,* a *world round-about.* Interpreted on the basis of their significance, these environs open up an understanding of the factical spatiality from out of which and on the basis of which the space of nature and geometrical space originally arise by means of a certain shift in our way of looking at it. It is on the basis of factical spatiality that we can define the ontological meaning of *being "in"* [Seins *"in"*] the environs of the world.

This "being" itself is what is encountering the world and indeed in such a manner that it is in the world as what it is concerned about and attends to, as a worldly being-there [*Weltdasein*]. It is characterized by *caring,* a fundamental mode of being which is distinctive in that it *"is"* its world, the very world it has encountered. This being — *being a worldly being-there which it is concerned about and attends to* — is a mode of the being-there of factical life.

The apparent difficulty of untangling this context of tightly interwoven categories and demonstrating it in intuition will disappear if from start to finish our treatment of it is required always anew to hold to the task of appropriating the corresponding position of looking at it and holding out in this looking to the very end, i.e., staying clear of a certain sedimented customary approach and being on guard against slipping back into it unawares.

What is first needed is a straightforward presentation of *what* the world is encountered *as* and indeed, corresponding to our forehaving, what it

---

1. Preview at the end of a class.

is being encountered *as* in the initial givens now and soon to come which are closest to us in the awhileness of the temporal particularity of an average everydayness. This awhileness refers to a circumscribed situation in which everydayness finds itself, circumscribed by initial and temporally particular givens which are closest to us and are there for a while in a certain "whiling" or "tarrying awhile" at home in them.

This *tarrying awhile* at home in . . . has its while, its character of a measured sojourn and holding out in the *temporality* of everydayness, a tarrying awhile at home in . . . which stretches along a span of temporality.[57] This tarrying awhile is initially and for the most part not the kind of tarrying in which we merely observe something. Rather, it is a being-occupied with something or other at the moment. Halting on the street can indeed be an idle standing around, but even as this kind of sojourn it is still something completely different than the occurrence of a thing called "man" between other things called "houses" or "rows of houses." Tarrying awhile in the sense of an idle standing around can only be understood as something temporalizing itself within a for-the-most-part-tarrying-awhile which consists in being-on-the-way to something (in a "being concerned about and attending to" in an especially pronounced sense).

What was said above was intended to lead us in the direction of bringing a concrete situation phenomenally into view in accord with the stretches of the awhileness of its temporal particularity and having a look at how, in this awhileness as the how of the everydayness which is closest to us, the world is being encountered. Here we need to be cautioned against a widespread error which consists in taking a so-called "experience" [*Erlebnis*] in the sense of an isolated act, an artificial extract, as it were, from life, to be so-called "straightforward" or "plain experience" [*Erfahrung*], in which what is experienced is in turn supposed to unlock the meaning of the being-there of things and of reality in general.

§19. An inaccurate description of the everyday world

In order to bring an authentic analysis into sharper relief and at the same time to characterize the kind of disastrous mistakes which are easily made in such primitive descriptions, an inaccurate description can initially be given, and indeed one which is not a fabrication and affectation on our part, but rather the one which everyone would today happily have pass for the most unbiased and straightforward description of what is immediately given and which is made the foundation of all subsequent descriptions of the so-called structural relations in an object. However, this description is still far superior to all those theories which tell stories about the transcendence of objects and reality without ever having taken a look at the matters so valiantly written about.

The purest everydayness can be called on: tarrying for a while at home, being-in-a-room, where eventually "a table" is encountered! As what is it being encountered? A thing in space—as a spatial thing, it is also a material thing. It has such and such a weight, such and such a color, such and such a shape, with a rectangular or round top—so high, so wide, with a smooth or rough surface. The thing can be dismantled, burned, or dissolved in some other way. This material thing in space which offers itself to possible sensation from different directions always shows itself as being-there only from a certain side and indeed in such a way that the aspect seen from one side flows over in a continuous manner into other aspects sketched out in advance in the spatial gestalt of the thing, and the same holds for these ones. Aspects show themselves and open up in ever new ways as we walk around the thing—and still others when we look down on it from above or perceive it from below. The aspects themselves change according to lighting, distance, and similar factors bound up with the position of the perceiver.

The being-there-in-such-a-manner of this thing which is given "in the flesh" provides the possibility of determining something about the meaning of the being of such objects and their being-real. In the proper sense, such objects are stones and other similar things in nature. However, when seen more closely, the table is also something more—it is not only a material thing in space, but in addition is furnished with definite valuative predicates: beautifully made, useful—it is a piece of equipment, furniture, a part of the room's decor. The total domain of what is real can accordingly be divided into two realms: *things in nature* and *things of value*—and the latter always contain the being of a natural thing as the basic stratum of their being. The authentic being of the table is: material thing in space.

When seen in terms of their results, these descriptions are apparently true, but only apparently. It can be shown that they are in numerous ways constructivistic and stand under the dominance of almost ineradicable *prejudices*. In demonstrating this, it would also become clear that if, as is now gradually becoming customary, one were to ascribe an original equality to the being of things invested with value and the being of those invested with meaning, this would still change nothing, so long as a fundamental lack of clarity prevailed *about* how these things are encountered, *about* the right position of looking in which something can be found out about them, and *about* the fact that significance is not a characteristic of things, but a characteristic of being.

Theories about actuality and reality need to be subjected to a critical phenomenological destruction from four points of view. These can be listed here without fully discussing them, especially since such a critique is able to be actualized only from out of positive insight. What needs to be shown is (1) why significance is not as such seen; (2) why it is that, even though an aspect of illusion is theoretically attributed to it, significance is still considered to be something which requires explanation and accordingly is explained; (3) why it is "explained" by dissolving it into a more primordial being-real; and (4) why this authentic founding being is sought in the being of things in nature. (Always-being-there, lawfulness, noncontingency—a flight into the subsistence of what is known, i.e., of what is meant by beings—ἐπιστήμη [science].)

§20. *A description of the everyday world on the basis of going about dealings in which we tarry for a while*

Nothing at all of what was mentioned in the first description given above is found in going about dealings[58] in which we concretely tarry for a while—and if something of it can be, then it will be in a different manner. Considered solely in terms of raw subject matter, the "same" example will be held onto and a new description carried out in such a manner that initially a multiplicity of related phenomena will become visible before the phenomenal context which relates them does. That is something which subsequent analysis will bring into relief.

What is there in *the* room there at home is *the* table (not "a" table among many other tables in other rooms and houses) at which one sits *in order to* write, have a meal, sew, play. Everyone sees this right away, e.g., during a visit: it is a writing table, a dining table, a sewing table—such is the primary way in which it is being encountered in itself. This characteristic of "in order to do something" is not merely imposed on the table by relating and assimilating it to something else which it is not.

Its standing-there in the room means: Playing this role in such and such characteristic use. This and that about it is "impractical," unsuitable. That part is damaged. It now stands in a better spot in the room than before—there's better lighting, for example. Where it stood before was not at all good (for . . .). Here and there it shows lines—the boys like to busy themselves at the table. These lines are not just interruptions in the paint, but rather: it was the boys and it still is. This side is not the east side, and this narrow side so many cm. shorter than the other, but rather the one at which my wife sits in the evening when she wants to stay up and read, there at the table we had such and such a discussion that time, there that decision was made with a *friend* that time, there that *work* written that time, there that *holiday* celebrated that time.

That is *the* table—as such is it there in the temporality of everydayness, and as such will it perhaps happen to be encountered again after many years when, having been taken apart and now unusable, it is found lying on the floor somewhere, just like other "things," e.g., a plaything, worn out and almost unrecognizable—it is my youth. In a corner of the basement stands an old pair of skis, the one is broken in half—what stands there are not material things of different lengths, but rather the skis from that time, from that daredevil trip with so and so. That book over there was a gift from X, that one there was bound by such and such a bookbinder, this other one needs to be taken to *him* soon, with that one I have been wrestling for a long time, that one there was an *unnecessary* buy, a flop, I still need to read this one for the first time. My library is not as good as A's but far better than B's, this matter is not something one would be able to derive pleasure from, what will the others say about this way of doing it, and the like. These are characteristics of the world's being-encountered. What now needs to be inquired into is how they constitute the being-there of the world.

Of the two descriptions, the first was characterized as an inaccurate description, i.e., with respect to the basic task posed: ontologically and categorially grasping the immediate givens closest to us in the beings-which-are-there. This does not mean it is "false," as if it had no basis in the subject matter. It is possible for the essential content of its results to prove itself vis-à-vis a specific domain of being-there to be *objectively* there for a theoretical observing which has a definite direction and focus.

Like all traditional ontology and logic, the first description stands within the unchecked sphere of influence of *the* fate which with Parmenides was decided for our intellectual history and the history of our Dasein, i.e., for the tendency of their interpretation: τὸ γὰρ αὐτὸ νοεῖν ἐστίν τε καὶ εἶναι, "perceptual mean-ing[59] and being are the same."[1] (Nonetheless, this statement needs to be kept free from other interpretations which are uncritical in their hermeneutical foundations insofar as they approach it as the first fundamental insight of idealism: all beings are what they are as constituted in thinking, consciousness—the object in the subject.) What is perceived in perceptual mean-ing is nothing other than beings-which-are-there in the authentic sense, i.e., authentic being has as its appropriate mode of access and apprehension perceptual mean-ing, "thinking," theoretical apprehension, science, and is for the Greeks "what is always already there" as such (By the way: intentionality—no accident that today Husserl is still characterizing the intentional as the "noetic.").

All subsequent ontology was defined in advance from out of this and guided by it. Recovering a primordial situation presupposes a critique of the development of this intellectual history.

---

1. Fr. 5 (Fr. 3 in the new enumeration) in Diels, *Vorsokratiker,* Vol. 1 (Berlin, 3d ed., 1912), p. 152.

Chapter Four

Significance as the Character of the
World's Being-Encountered

*§21. An analysis of significance
(first version, not delivered in the course)*

Our description was carried out intentionally with a view to providing
an indication of only those modes of the being-encountered of "things"
which are found in a certain circumscribed occasion of their being-encountered, one which is, however, for the most part and for most of us
something close to us and a given. The *as-what* and how of their being-
encountered can be designated as *significance*—and this itself interpreted
as a category of being. "Significant" means: being, being-there, in the
how of a definite signifying and pointing[60]—what this means, that
wherein its definiteness consists, and how in all this a *being*-there announces itself is what now needs to be brought into relief from out of
the concrete.

The *definiteness* of this signifying, which is what initially needs to be
explicated, lies in the characteristic of the *disclosedness* of that which is
for a while significant to us at the particular time in question.[61] (Disclosedness—not merely the *definiteness* of definitions in the realm of
knowledge—the latter is a special dimension of sight and *as such* one
which is also still *average*. Being-interpreted moves around in it.) This
disclosedness shows itself in two basic characteristics: (1) the characteristic
of availability in advance, (2) the characteristic of the advance appearance of a with-world (i.e., bringing-about-the-appearance of those with
us in the world, holding them in this appearance).[62]

1. In the above description,[63] what is being encountered in a "worldly"
manner shows itself as being a means to . . . , used to . . . , no longer really
suitable for . . . , no longer used to . . . : its being-there is a being-*there-
for-this*. "There-in-order-to-do-this" means: ready-to-hand for *being-occupied with* . . . , for a tarrying for a while in it from out of which arises this
or that looking around for it to do something with it, this or that position-
ing in relation to. . . . What is there in such being-there-ready-to-hand as
such, and there as something well-known and disclosed, is the *in-order-to*,
and this in the mode of being of a definite everyday being-*in-such-and-
such-a-manner*—e.g., in order to have a meal (this alone or with definite
others and at different times of the day). Even *this definite everydayness and
temporality* are thus *available in advance*. Already having been there in such
and such a manner and expected to be there again in such and such a

manner. Past and future as definite horizons which each define the present—pressing forth into the there[64] from out of the past and future. (Temporality: there from that time, for, during, for the sake of.

Paths of being concerned about and attending to.[65] The beings-which-are-there do not stand within the definiteness of definitions, but rather within that of everydayness and its historicity, e.g., the books coming forth for a while at particular times [*jeweilen herkünftig*] from out of the "intensity" of anxious concern and its apprehensions[66]: not yet, to be . . . for the first time, already, but only for nothing—"no longer" serves as means to, "stands, lies around," "in the way," junk—the "there." In dealings, the going-toward, gaining-access-to, and going-around which lets something be encountered, a being-open: for disclosedness and the forehaving of caring from out of *everydayness* and for it.)

2. Available in advance in such a manner, the there in advance brings about the appearance of "the others" in its being-*there*, a definite sphere of those with us in life which defines itself from out of everydayness—whoever these definite others happen to be: he who gave me the book, the carpenter who made the table, he who has a better library in the area of. . . .

What shows itself in the expression "it was the boys" *by becoming explicit in the past* is there in an inexplicit, to one degree or another obvious, and indistinct manner in each and every thing being encountered in the above worldly manner: for the most part—and precisely as something utterly smoothed over and self-evident—*"one-self,"* [67] one's own temporality in its everydayness. What one pursues, that wherein one tarries for a while—one-self "is" this world. Whatever one-self is, one is it in the world with the others—it defines itself from out of and on the basis of what one in advance comes to appearance as with the others and in contrast to *them*. The everydayness of Dasein has its Dasein there for itself and seeks it on the path of heeding what the others say about it, what its pursuits look like to the others, how *the others in advance come to appearance within its pursuits.*

Even there where the disclosedness of what is being encountered—the in-order-to, the for-whom, the from-whom, etc.—is not encountered in the *familiarity* of the everyday (the possibilities of familiarity are factically historical), where something *strange* presses into the world closest to us and we happen across it, the characteristic of disclosedness nonetheless announces itself precisely there in our exploring the thing in question from certain points of view as we tarry at it for a while—the question "what is it?" explicates itself into a "What is it for? What are we supposed to do with it? Who is it for? What is it supposed to be? Who made it?"

What, in that which is being encountered, constitutes its disclosedness is so little a multiplicity of relations into which the encountered beings-which-are-there are subsequently and secondarily placed that it is rather precisely *from out of* and *on the basis of* this *disclosedness* that what is being encountered is *there*, holds itself in its being-there, and lingers in it (Here "relations" take the form of environs, the round-about). The beings-which-are-there in everydayness are not beings which already *are* in an authentic sense *prior to* and *apart from* their "in order to do something" and their "for someone," but rather their being-*there* lies precisely in this "in order to" and "for," and where this, the disclosedness, breaks down, then it is *it* which breaks down—i.e., even then are the beings in question still there in *it:* the beings are *there* and for our being-occupied (going about dealings) "they stand in the way."

Something existing in the mode of an occurring object we simply take note of, observe, and ascertain can be *there* for us only as a being-there in everydayness, only that in this case it has forfeited the authentic character of its there and now holds itself in and lingers in the indifference of something we are merely able to ascertain. But such ascertainability is not its being, but rather the possibility of its being-an-object—in contrast, the disclosedness of what has significance shows the latter in the how of its *being*-there. (The genesis of the theoretical, what is prior here: "curiosity.")

From out of and *by way of* the disclosedness being encountered in it and as it, what has significance signifies itself and points itself into the "there" of a particular tarrying-for-a-while and situation of everydayness. What has significance and points in this manner signifies not something else but itself and is signific*ant*, i.e., it *holds itself* in this being-there and being-available, *lingering* in them in accord with the awhileness of temporal particularity in question and throughout it.

The pertinacity of established epistemological theories which are constructivistic not only generally, but also specifically regarding what they single out in advance as their subject matter and generate constructions about, namely, theoretical perceiving and knowing, can make the phenomena exhibited above seem quite strange initially. The pertinacity of such theories and the apparent strangeness of the analysis can be clarified with regard to what motivates them only on the basis of developing *that* kind of seeing in which significance is encountered. Significance can only be understood on the basis of the disclosedness which is found in it and from out of which *what is being encountered* signifies itself through a pointing within the other things we encounter and in this way presses forth into its there. (In dealings, the going-toward, gaining-access-to, and going-around which lets something be encountered, a being-open for disclosedness in the forehaving of caring from out of everydayness and for it.)

§22. An analysis of significance[1] (second version)

Our indicative description was intentionally carried out with a view to providing an indication of the modes of the being-encountered and being-there of "mere things." It is precisely this phenomenal horizon of looking which we will continue to hold fast, though this does not have the sense of limiting us to a certain domain which has been singled out, but rather is being done with a view to a purpose which is of fundamental and far-reaching importance regarding method. What will shortly be brought to light is precisely what is going on in the worldly being-there of mere things (table, books) on an ontological level.

As a derivation from "world," the term "worldly" is not to be understood as the opposite of "in the mind," but rather means in formal terms: to be there as "world." The character of the being-there of this world can be terminologically designated as *significance*. "Significant" means: being, being-there, in the mode of a signifying which is being encountered in a definite manner. This expression does not refer to a being-which-is-there which, in addition to being there, also signifies something—what constitutes its being is rather precisely its signifying which is being encountered in a definite manner, its holding itself in this signifying and lingering in it. We therefore need to explain that and how significance constitutes this worldly *being-there*.

Our analysis has two parts and touches on the following:
1. Signifying and its phenomenal contexts (§§23-25).
2. Its being-encountered which is characterized in a definite manner (the character of the world's being-encountered) (§26).
Signifying will become visible in the following three phenomena:
1. disclosedness (§23),
2. familiarity (§24),
3. the unpredictable and comparative (§25).

§23. Disclosedness

The phenomenon of disclosedness is articulated into two unified characteristics:
   (a) availability in advance,
   (b) the advance appearance of the with-world.

---

1. Delivered in the course. H.'s heading.

A. Availability

What is being encountered is there as "a means to," "useful for," "of importance for." Its being-*there* is based on its being-there-in-order-to-do-this and being-there-for-this. It is ready-to-hand from out of and on the basis of its definite there-in-order-to-do-this and there-for-this. This being-ready-to-hand, being-at-our-disposal, constitutes its *availability in advance*. The definiteness of the there-in-order-to-do-this and that of the there-for-this are not merely applied to and predicated of beings-which-are-there [*Da-seienden*] initially without them, but rather the reverse: precisely they are what is primary and what for the very first time presses what we encounter forth into its authentic encountered being-there [*Da-sein*] and holds it enclosed in this being-there.

If we are to gain a correct understanding of the phenomenal structure of *availability in advance*, it is important to *see* that the in-order-to and for-what make up the originally given "there" which is closest to us and not to *explain* them as something we come across subsequently in the sense of an external point of view imposed on and affixed to what is already there. The in-order-to and for-what (the daily meals, the habits of writing and working, sewing from time to time, playing from time to time) are not just arbitrary, free-floating modes of being-occupied at the table and tarrying for a while at it, but rather ones which are defined in the awhileness of their temporal particularity from out of a historical everydayness, defining and redefining themselves anew *from out of* such everydayness and *for* it in ways cut to the measure of its temporality. (Important for the "whereto" of being-out-for and going-toward: fore-care and its "about," what it goes "around" in.)[68] *How care's being-encountered-in-advance in an inexplicit manner is motivated in availability in advance and how care contributes precisely to the authentic character of the there of what we encounter will be shown in the analysis of the character of the world's being-encountered.* Availability in advance defines the peculiar character of the there: being in a co-encountered ownmost there-in-order-to-do-this and there-for-this.

B. The appearance of the with-world

What is being encountered is what it is and how it is as "*the* table there in the room" at which *we* (one and indeed a definite "one") have our daily meals, at which that discussion was launched into that time, that game played, in which those definite people *were there* and were involved, i.e., *are* still also there in the being-there [*Da-sein*] of this table there in the room—as that book over there, the one which was a gift from X, the one which was poorly bound by bookbinder B, etc. One pursues a matter as something which is intended to look like such and such to the others, be a success in their eyes, outdo them.

Others—definite others who are defined at particular times and for a while [*jeweilen*] from out of temporality—are there in what is being encountered in everydayness in the above manner. Initially and for the most part, those with us in life and close by, those-who-are-there-with-us in everydayness, do not turn up in an isolated explicitness, but rather in advance come to appearance precisely in what one pursues, in what one is occupied with. Being there in such appearance does not at all mean being the object of a knowing which is directed to it—rather the appearance of a with-world takes place in advance in availability (the for-what and in-order-to), such that it in like manner presses those-who-are-there from out of it and on the basis of it forth into their there.

The advance appearance of the factical lives of others in what is being encountered is more closely defined by the fact that this appearance is *"in a with-world,"* i.e., the factical lives of others are being encountered in a "worldly" manner: as those one "has something to do with," those one works with, plans something with (the many others who are "immaterial" for all this and on account of it)—"with" insofar as they are others in such a manner that "one-self" has something to do with them.

They are encountered in this "with"-world in such a manner that these others bring with them the *"one-self."* In the appearance of those who are being encountered in a with-world, one-self is therewith what one pursues, "one-self," one's status, reputation, accomplishments, successes and failures among the others. In the there of the table and other such "things" which are being encountered, one is one-self therewith in an inexplicit manner what is being encountered. And this not—and even less so than in the case of the others—in the sense of something grasped theoretically or in some other explicit manner. And above all one-self is there in this manner without any self-observation turning back upon an ego, without reflection—on the contrary, one encounters one-self in this being-occupied with the world in dealings.

§24. Familiarity

The phenomenal whole of disclosedness, from out of which and on the basis of which something being encountered in a factical manner signifies and points itself into its there, is itself a peculiar context of references. The how of *such*[1] referential signifying is encountered in terms of the characteristic of a *familiarity* with it which prevails for a

---

1. H.'s n.: "How? more precision!!"

while at the particular time.[69] The advance availability of what we encounter and the advance appearance of those whom we encounter in a with-world are well-known (ἕξις [state of having, habit], ἀλήθεια [truth, uncoveredness]), and this not in the sense of having knowledge of and about them, but rather in the sense that they are the wherein in which *one*, corresponding to what and who is to be encountered, knows one's way around, one-self. Everydayness thoroughly dominates the definite relations in these contexts of reference. Each knows his way around for a while at the particular time, knows others well, just as these others know him well.[70] This being-well-known in the with-world is one which is average, thriving in everydayness and developing into its contentments. This familiarity is not simply a characteristic of comprehension, but rather a mode of the being-encountered of the beings-which-are-there themselves, being-"in."

§25. The unpredictable and comparative

Only on the basis of this familiarity can something *"strange"* come forth within the initial givens of the there of the world which are closest to us—it is something unfamiliar, "stands in the way," "comes at an inconvenient time," "is uncomfortable," "disturbing," "awkward," hindering.[71] As such, it has in the character of its there a pronounced oppressiveness, a heightened "there." This possibility of the intensification of the character of the there of something which comes down on us like a storm or is already there as an inconvenience lies right within the *inexplicit* self-evidence of the familiarity of the there of the everyday world.[1]

The strange is only this inexplicit familiarity insofar as it has been shaken up and awakened and is now being encountered in the character of unfamiliarity. This lack of familiarity is not merely something occasional, but rather belongs to the very temporality of the world's being-encountered. The familiarity is disturbed, and this disturbable familiarity is what gives to the contingent "otherwise than one thought" the recalcitrant sense of its there.

Through the disturbability of inexplicit familiarity, what is being encountered is there in its *unpredictability*, its *incalculability*. The there encountered has the peculiar rigidity of something oppressive, contingent. This for-the-most-part-some-how-otherwise pervades the world's being-encountered—it is comparative: otherwise than one thought, planned, etc.

---

1. What follows is again a student transcript, since one or two pages are missing at the end of H.'s manuscript. See Editor's Epilogue.

§26. The character of the world's being-encountered

We can be sure of having gained a clear view of this last-mentioned characteristic and the others previously described only after the character of the being-encountered of the beings-which-are-there has itself been defined.

These beings-which-are-there are being encountered in the how of their being-of-concern, i.e., in their there which has been placed into *concern*. In its pronounced sense, being-of-concern and being-attended-to means being-finished: when care has finished with it and made it ready, when it stands there at our disposal—precisely then is it for the first time something we are concerned about and attend to in the proper sense.

The being-there which is being encountered has its own *temporality*, and this is something we are concerned about and attend to in a broader sense. What we are concerned about and attend to is there as not yet, as to be . . . for the first time, as already, as approaching, as until now, as for the time being, as finally.[72] These may be designated as *kairological* moments of being-there. It is only on the basis of this temporality that all the basic moments of time can be understood.

In order to understand the phenomenal context of significance, it is necessary to see that its disclosedness stands in the respective kind of *care* which tarries for a while at the particular time.[73] The multiplicity of references is nothing other than that wherein [*worin*] concern holds itself and sojourns. In advance of this, that about which [*worum*] care is concerned, that wherein it goes around, is the for-what [*Wofür*] and in-order-to [*Wozu*] and the others in the with-world which are found in them.[74] What it is concerned about and attends to is the context of references itself.

This going-here-and-there in the context of references is what characterizes *caring* as a *going about dealings* in the sense of a *going around*.[75] The context of references is the environs in the authentic sense, the round-about. Significance must be defined ontologically as the with-which [*Womit*] of dealings with it which is there in our being concerned about it, attending to it, and going around in it. It is from out of and on the basis of this "round-about" that the factically spatial environing world is sustained in its being-there-in-such-and-such-a-manner.

Spatiality, which is saturated in a factical manner with concern, has its distances—it is there as: too far, nearby, through this street, through the kitchen, a stone's throw, behind the cathedral, and the like. In this spatiality is found a familiarity with its references which prevails for a while at the particular time,[76] and these references are always those of concern.

In its primary ontological sense, the "round-about" is not at all defined by a being-located-side-by-side-and-around-each-other and by geometrical relations, but rather it is the round-about of worldly dealings with it which are concerned about it, attend to it, and go around in it. It provides the possibility of rightly interpreting the ontological meaning of being-"in"-a-world and being-"within"-a-world. To-be-"in"-the-world does not mean occurring among other things, but rather: all the while being concerned about it and attending to it, tarrying awhile "at home in" the round-about of the world being encountered. The authentic mode of "being" in a world is *caring*[77] in the sense of producing, putting in place, directing ourselves to tasks, taking into possession, preventing, protecting against loss, etc. Environs, the round-about, are the averageness of life, its open space of publicness. In its caring, life approaches itself and addresses itself in a worldly manner.

Looking back on what was said about the advance appearance of the with-world, what came to light was: In the there we are concerned about and attend to, *what we are concerned about and attend to* is the with-world and with this *one-self*. Its basic character is defined by this: with what it is out for, whereto it is going, it places itself into care. Caring is always concerned about itself and attends to itself in some manner. (This is not a reflexivity of caring back upon itself, this is not what we are talking about.) Caring is concerned about itself and attends to itself in that it meets up with itself in a worldly manner in the there it is encountering. Caring as such is precisely what originally has the world there and puts temporality in place in such a manner that the world is something being encountered in caring and for it. The importance of this fundamental phenomenon should not in any way be underestimated.

Being in the how of such caring is *anxious concern and its apprehensions*. This characterizes life as a being-placed into a world, one which is concerned about the world and attends to it in its dealings with it. Caring is "being"-in-a-world and should not be interpreted as an act of consciousness.

The far-reaching importance of our methodical way of proceeding in which the analysis remained at the level of mere things can now be seen in the fact that in the dealings of everyday life which are closest to us the environing world, the world round-about, is always there also as a with-world and a self-world. These terms do not demarcate regions over against each other, but rather are definite modes of the world's being-encountered—each displays the specific character of the round-about. These environs are nothing other than averageness, the open space of publicness. (Everything here simply condensed, from the point of view of the analyses of the today.)

Life is there in everydayness as the world it is encountering, as the world which it is concerned about and attends to and which is met up with in caring. Life is concerned about itself and attends to itself and all the while—since care has in each particular case a language—addresses itself in a worldly manner.[78]

What lies in the character of the being of care is that it becomes absorbed in its temporalization, in its actualization. Care disappears in the habits, customs, and publicness of everydayness—and this does not mean it comes to an end, but rather that it does not show itself any longer, it is covered up. Being-concerned-about and going about dealings have the immediate aspect of *carefreeness*. The world being encountered appears as simply there in a straightforward manner.

In the leveled-off there of this carefreeness which concernfully attends to the world, a world encountered in this carefreeness as something self-evident, care is asleep. On account of this, the possibility ever remains that distress will suddenly break forth in the world. The world can be encountered as something distressing only insofar as it is a world which is of significance to us.

(I must break off at this point.) What needs to be explained on the basis of the character of the being-there of the world which has been defined is in what way *curiosity* (*cura* [care]—*curiositas* [curiosity]!) is a *how of caring*. How curiosity in its explicit actualization does not do away with the self-evidence of the being-there of Dasein, but rather reinforces it. It can do this because the care of curiosity constantly covers itself up [*sich selbst verdeckt*]. The four characteristics of self-interpretation previously mentioned[1] are the masquerades of curiosity by means of which it hides [*sich verdeckt*] from its own care. Spranger's "all of us" is only a masking of uncertainty and insecurity: no one has seen it, no one believes it, each is too cowardly to admit it.

The phenomenon of *care* must be seen as a *fundamental phenomenon of the being-there of Dasein*. It is not something which can be pieced together out of theoretical, practical, emotional components. What first needs to be clarified on the basis of this phenomenon is that it is in the being-there of caring itself, understood in its primordiality prior to any attempt to break it apart, that the care of mere seeing and mere questioning is grounded in the being of human existence.

1. See pp. 49–50 above.

Appendix: Inserts and Supplements

(All headings for these inserted pages are by H.)

I.
Investigations for a hermeneutics
of facticity (1-1-1924) [regarding §§15, 19-20]

Unobtrusively putting a rigorous research plan[79] forth in concrete investigations—i.e., doing this from out of and on the basis of a primordial
kind of comportment only just now obtained. End: hermeneutical situation (itself research!)—questionableness.

For the concrete investigations, each in its place and at a particular time
[*jeweils*]: historical investigations—Aristotle, Augustine, Parmenides. (Hermeneutics is destruction!) Only in such a manner demonstrating the
primordiality of this hermeneutical destructive research.
Themes:[80]
A. Facticity—ontology—being—the awhileness of temporal particularity—Dasein in its being-there: each related to hermeneutics. The decisive
historical dimension: beginning each of the investigations on the basis
of initial givens which are closest to us and in each case doing this at a
particular time [*jeweils*] in a destructive concrete manner for such definite
investigations.

Should be forced by the concrete temporal particularity of the investigation to go back and make an explicit appropriation—true safeguarding against a system and a polished philosophy one adopts and opines.
Seeing more positively: researching of facticity in its historical necessity.

E. Hermeneutics of facticity: in going back to A., taking up a facticity
which is now radical.[81]

II.
Themes (1-1-1924) [regarding §§7-13]

The today. cf. Ontology, i.e., philosophy: Platonism, curiosity.
As possibilities here
Husserl. Dilthey.
(with respect to not "names," but what is decisive regarding subject
matter)
What does such interpretation-with-respect-to-possibilities mean?[82]
Husserl: radicality! what kind? Subject matter, the how.

Descartes, care about known knowledge.
Greeks. (Truth (falsity) — uncoveredness.)
The today in historical consciousness:
Dilthey, laying a foundation,[83] cf. Husserl, Descartes, Greeks.

for it: traditional forehaving, psychology, idea of man, anthropology.
Aristotle — New Testament — Augustine — Luther.
On the basis of both forehaving and foreconception. Destruction of philosophy with the idea of research, hermeneutics of facticity.

The today and the "generation." In opposition to fantastic world-history. Instead on the ground, and let it be that of radical concrete questionableness.

III.

In overview[1] (1-1-1924) [regarding §§7-13, 14-15]

"Phenomenology" — λόγος [discourse] — ψεῦδος [false, covering up] — ἀληθές [true, uncovering]. Cares — "problems" — questions, consciousness as thematic field.
Seizing upon uncoveredness — being-there, etc.
Taking our orientation *not* primarily from a discipline — "phenomenology" — but from being and indeed the being-there of Dasein and this concretely as the awhileness of temporal particularity, today. (cf. SS 23 Ontology.) Point of departure in the today still more concrete — our own research, on account of the radicality of the object and its obstruction.
Historical consciousness — philosophy — religion and theology.

1. Here at the same time being in earnest about phenomenology as a possibility,

2. at the same time Dilthey subjected to destruction — authentic "reality of life" — with this, by means of 1., the historical in a radical sense. Greek ontology — idea of man — Christian theology, Augustine — destruction! Going back to Greek ontology, starting from the idea of man — λόγος — science — validity — Descartes — the care of curiosity and for validity and certainty. Publicness.
Or precisely phenomenology as a how of the today and indeed the concrete possibility of coming to an end and radically going *back* — proceeding from the start only in terms of subject matter.

---

1. Remark added later by Heidegger: "'Introduction' Marburg WS 23-24 unsuccessful, usable only if rigorously reworked." [For this lecture course from the winter semester of 1923-24 at the University of Marburg, see *Gesamtausgabe*, Vol. 17: *Einführung in die phänomenologische Forschung* (*Introduction to Phenomenological Research*) (Frankfurt: Klostermann, 1994).]

1-4-1924

With phenomenology in the sense of a discipline as the (initial) point of departure, reflectively stepping back from it and, by starting with it as a possibility, coming to a fundamental "subject matter" which bears within itself the very possibility of research and how to do it.

Should the "whereto" of proceeding turn out to be a decisive kind of possibility, then the fundamental meaning of Husserl's phenomenological discoveries would have to be demonstrated in concrete terms from out of it.

IV.
Hermeneutics and dialectic[2] *(regarding §9)*

Dialectic—historical destruction—understanding.
Forehaving—foreconception. Task of forehaving and foreign elements in foreconception: *idea of classification, curiosity.* "Truth," uncoveredness, development of the uncoveredness, and dialectic. Dialectic in being negated does not lead to and call for *direct* grasping and having. A more radical possibility, new conceptuality: hermeneutics.

V.
Human being [regarding §§4-5, 2, 14]

Concerning the presuppositions, conditions, motives (forehaving, foreconception) of *questioning,* of gaining access to *factical life.*

"To be a human being means to belong to a race endowed with reason, to belong to it as a specimen, so that the race or species is higher than the individual, which is to say that there are no individuals, only specimens" (Ki., *Attack [on Christendom],* 461).[3]

Inadequate efforts of *"philosophy of life"* with respect to its tendency of articulation. In contrast, the polemic *against* philosophy of life loses sight of everything, does not in any way see the object "life" in a primordial manner, does not see the problem of forehaving. Thus its polemic against lack of conceptuality is purely negative, i.e., "positively" misguided and caught in a void.

---

2. H.'s heading with the added remark: "cf. lecture course, SS 23, regarding p. 9 [of the manuscript]" (i.e., dialectic).

3. I.e., Kierkegaard, *Kierkegaards Angriff auf die Christenheit,* ed. A. Dorner and C. Schrempf (1896), Vol. I, p. 461. [*The Point of View for My Work as an Author,* trans. Walter Lowrie (New York: Harper & Brothers, 1962), p. 111 (modified).]

"Sojourning at home in . . . and holding out there," a mode of actualizing and temporalizing. Philosophy and indeed philosophical research is only a definite kind of sojourning at home in . . . , the most radical questionableness—and this in its interpretation as factically concrete in the context of life prevailing for a while at the particular time.[84]

The development of concrete sojourns and abodes in life—the productive logic of the sciences.

The Greek sojourn and its doctrine of being. The how of the development of the sojourn—the how of the interpretation of the sojourn (from out of and on the basis of what kind of being). How the doctrine of being defines the sojourn and this a logic.

Hence at first calling on ontology for the task of destructive interpretation—and the reverse, i.e., a multifaceted possibility. And this means: facticity *is* what is primordial, and what is already equiprimordially found in it is a multiplicity of different movements and interpretations and objects. Reaching this primordial dimension right away and understanding its historical character.

VI.

Ontology. Natura hominis [*Nature of man*] [*regarding §§4-5, 13*]

"Quand tout se remue également, rien ne se remue en apparence, comme en un vaisseau. Quand tous vont vers le débordement, nul n'y semble aller. Celui qui s'arrête fait remarquer l'emportement des autres, comme un point fixe." ["When all is equally moving, nothing appears to be moving, as on a ship. When all tend to excess, none appears to do so. He who halts draws attention to how the others are carried away, as if he were a fixed point.][4]

It is mistaken to be out to participate in movement as such—especially if this is done with a view to being able to see the movement of life and bring it into the forehaving of categorial explication as an object. We are able to see *movement* in an authentic manner only from out of a genuine *"sojourn"* in which we hold out for a while at the particular time.[85] Existential sojourn, in this sojourn—what is to be fixed on as standing still? And thus the most important task: precisely winning a genuine sojourn and not just any kind—the sojourn *before* the *possibility* of leaping into the work of worried decision—not talked about, but it is constantly there. Motion is visible in the sojourn and from out of this the possibility of countermovement as the genuine way to sojourn.

Sojourning and holding out in life itself, in the meaning of its being

4. B. Pascal, *Pensées et Opuscules*, ed. L. Brunschvicg (Paris, no date), Section VI, No. 382, p. 503. [*Thoughts, Letters, Minor Works*, trans. W. F. Trotter et al. (New York: P. F. Collier & Son, 1910), p. 128 (modified).]

and of its being an object: facticity. Holding back from a ruinous movement, i.e., being in earnest about the difficulty involved, actualizing the
wakeful intensification of the difficulty which goes with this, bringing it
into true safekeeping.

VII.
The initial engagement and bringing into play[5] (regarding §3, p. 14)

The initial engagement and bringing into play, "as what" facticity is
grasped in advance and stirred, i.e., the decisive character of its being
which is initially put forth and brought into play, is not something which
can be fabricated, but rather arises out of a fundamental experience and
indeed here this means one which is philosophical, i.e., out of the truth
of a primordial self-interpretation of philosophy. In hermeneutics, it is
precisely the character of this initial engagement and bringing into play
which comes into view—moreover, Dasein itself becomes wide-awake
for this, i.e., for itself.

Here we find no discussion and debate, only evasion, flight, and
interpreting according to pretexts of meaning. An inconsequential academic enterprise in which, contrary to the meaning of science, one dares
to claim the prerogative of never having to know anything in a fundamental manner. One calls that: uncovering essential laws! The horrid
wretchedness of such systematic seduction of our fellow human beings.
Passing off presuppositions as something innocuous by means of formalistic rationalization and placing them before the public in this manner.

VIII.
Consummation [regarding Foreword]

1. Showing the exhaustion, (creative activity—is this what it all comes to?)
2. showing it to have increased in exhausted and forced neo-culture.

IX.
Phenomenology (regarding §9, p. 37)

That one treats *phenomenology* in this manner is in part its own fault. One
confuses its experiments and initial results with its authentic tendency,
which does not stand in full view and cannot simply be learned.

---

5. The ms. of this insert crossed out by H.

Göttingen 1913: for a whole semester Husserl's students argued about how a mailbox looks. Using this kind of treatment, one then moves on to talk about religious experiences as well. If that is philosophy, then I, too, am all for dialectic.

X.

Homo iustus [*The just man*] [*regarding §§4-5*]

Homo iustus—*rectus*—*bona voluntas*—*charitas dei* [*the just man*—righteous—good will—love of God]. Thus: *homo primus in gratia conditus est* [the first man was fashioned in grace], i.e., *in beata vita constitutus* [placed in a life of blessedness], see *De lib. arb.*, cap. 11 *in fine*.[6]

Formal deduction: *faciamus hominem* [let us make man]—forehaving about *man*! Redemption there—the more primordially and absolutely it is received, the more weight must sin carry. It carries it only insofar as the Fall is an absolute Fall, i.e.: the first "from which," the ἀρχή [origin], is the absolute *gratia Dei* [grace of God]. The τέλος [end]: pure sinfulness.

This back-and-forth relation is grounded in the forehaving: *man*, creature of God, in his image and likeness.

See especially Paul: glory of Χριστός [Christ] as the Redeemer—the exile of humanity into distress and death! The *death* of Christ—the problem! Experience of death in any sense, death—life—Dasein (Kierkegaard).

XI.

On Paul [*regarding §§4-5*]

Flesh-*spirit* (see *Religion in History and the Present*[7]): to be in them, a *how* as a "what," objective-heavenly, the *what* as the how of a history coming to an end. Explication of facticity: of the unredeemed and being-redeemed: υἱοί θεοῦ [sons of God] (Rom. 8:14). Death-life, sin-righteousness, slavery-sonship (fundamental experiences! The decisive mover?), Christ the turning. "History of salvation" unclear!

---

6. Augustine, *De libero arbitrio*, in Migne, Vol. XXXII (Paris, 1845), Liber I, cap. 11, p. 1233f. [*On Free Choice of the Will*, trans. Anna S. Benjamin and L. H. Hackstaff (New York: Macmillan, 1964), p. 23 (modified).]

7. *Religion in Geschichte und Gegenwart*, Vol. II (Tübingen, 3d ed., 1958), pp. 974-77.

XII.
Signifying (regarding §22)

A pointing both signified and signifying: being concerned about and attending to. . . . Something signifies something: lifts it up into a definite context of references, defines itself from out of beings, it is there. Conduciveness. Being concerned about and attending to . . . lets that which points and is signified be encountered as a being, in its being-there [*Da-sein*]. Concerned about the world and attending to it, being- *"in"* finds this world before itself, grows, as it were, right into it: table, jug, plow, saw, house, garden, field, village, path.

Usability—something employed for something—in possession: produced out of . . . , the out-of-which itself—wood to be ordered. Grain, flour, bread. Context of references. Familiarity—smoothing over and the strange!

Environs, the round-about . . . , place, space, from . . . to. . . . Nature, walk, weather.

Danger of passing over this, thing, from there and back (affixing). Above all not the character of the there, being. "The self-evidence of the there," absorption.

Editor's Epilogue

Käte Bröcker-Oltmanns

The text published here for the first time is Heidegger's lecture course "Ontology," which was held one hour a week (thirteen hours in all) in the summer semester of 1923. It was his last lecture course in Freiburg. In the winter semester, he assumed his appointment as Full Professor to the Distinguished Chair of Philosophy at the University of Marburg.

The title "Ontology," which is how Heidegger himself cited this course, is vague and accidental. The title of his planned course which he had originally submitted for the university catalogue was "Logic," and it was no doubt intended to be understood in the sense in which he was accustomed to use this technical term, i.e., as a "systematic" introduction to interpreting philosophical texts (cf. *Gesamtausgabe*, Vol. 61: *Phänomenologische Interpretationen zu Aristoteles* [Frankfurt: Klostermann, 1985], p. 183). But he had to change the title because another professor at the university also wanted to advertise a course called "Logic." He said, "Well, then 'Ontology.'" In the first hour of the course (see the "Introduction"), he then introduced the *real* title: "The Hermeneutics of Facticity." The course was then advertised on the notice board as "Ontology—The Hermeneutics of Facticity."[86]

This edition is based on Heidegger's own course manuscript which was written in Gothic script on 19 lengthwise folio pages (the text always on the left half and additional remarks and material for insertion on the right half) and also contained a series of inserts and supplements. A few of the separate pages added by Heidegger and mostly sketched somewhat later have been edited and presented in the Appendix.

A typewritten copy made by Dr. Hartmut Tietjen was at my disposal as a model for how to decipher the manuscript. It was compared word for word with the manuscript. Outside of a few necessary additions and corrections, I found it to be exceptional and gratefully made use of it.

Moreover, two student transcripts were at my disposal for this edition:

1. The transcript of my husband, Walter Bröcker, which was always copied out from shorthand into full manuscript form on the same day. It unfortunately went missing. The manuscript copy was years later borrowed by Herbert Marcuse and reproduced in typescript. Professor Rodi in Bochum was kind enough to make available a duplicate of it. He had acquired it for the Dilthey Archives from his teacher Professor Friedrich Bollnow in Tübingen. How the latter came into possession of it can no longer be determined. The original must be in the Marcuse Archives in Frankfurt.

The Marbach Literature Archives contains another copy of the manuscript form of Bröcker's transcript under the title "Transcript, W. Bröcker." This is a copy made by Karl Löwith for his personal use. He was not in Freiburg in the summer of 1923 but rather doing his doctorate in Munich.

2. From the Marbach Literature Archives I acquired a transcript by Helene Weiß which is also in manuscript form and was probably copied out from shorthand. It also contains additions from transcripts by others. Weiß was unfortunately not in Freiburg in July 1923 and thus heard only eight of the twelve hours of lectures (neither Bröcker nor Weiß was present at the first lecture in April). She filled out her transcript by copying three hours of lectures from the manuscript form of Bröcker's transcript. For the last hour of lecturing, she used two other dissimilar transcripts made by "Käte V" (Victorius) and someone unnamed.

The student transcripts were important for occasionally providing assistance in understanding passages in Heidegger's manuscript, but even more important for another difficulty in this edition: Heidegger's manuscript is incomplete. What is missing is (1) the lengthy "insert" referred to on page 14 of the manuscript (p. 52) and (2) one or two pages at the end of the course. The manuscript ends abruptly in the middle of Heidegger's train of thought.

1. The "insert" on phenomenon and phenomenology was not subsequently added to the manuscript of the course, since the following sentences immediately refer back to it. But it was also not written at the same time. Otherwise it would not have been skipped over in Heidegger's numbering of the manuscript pages. It was obviously inserted into the manuscript as an already finished text, then later taken out again for further use. Heidegger often gave talks on the theme it treats, doing so even in small circles. It was discussed fully in §7 of *Being and Time* and in his courses served above all, as it did here where he devoted more than two of the thirteen hours of lectures to it, to introduce his own path of philosophy (as it also did, for example, in his lecture course on Descartes the very next semester).

This is why Heidegger's extended remarks on the above theme could not have been left out at this point in the text. W. Bröcker's transcript was inserted as a substitute for this still-undiscovered part of the manuscript. Helene Weiß's transcript was used in supplementary fashion in the first section (up to p. 56, though without references). Regarding the remainder of Heidegger's remarks, her manuscript was unfortunately of no use (see above).

2. The removal of one or two pages at the end of the manuscript was surely not deliberate on Heidegger's part. They vanished in the course of the years, as easily happens, especially since the importance Heidegger attached to them was not the same as that which they have for us today.

W. Bröcker's transcript again had to be employed here as a substitute and was supplemented with a few things from the transcripts obtained through Helene Weiß.

The division of the text of the course into chapters and sections derives from the editor, as do the section headings. Where a heading is found in the manuscript, it is given in a footnote. The only other guides regarding the content of Heidegger's course are given in the table of contents, and it is intended in a certain sense to take the place of an index, which is something Heidegger absolutely did not want in his Collected Edition. The hasty reader can get an overview from it. The serious reader can disregard it.

I have also included in footnotes Heidegger's occasional marginal comments in the manuscript, which are mostly of a self-critical kind and which, because of the flow of the handwriting, clearly show themselves to have been added later. How much later cannot be determined. Like a few dated pages in the Appendix, they probably derive from the following winter.

Occasional stenographic notes in the manuscript had to be left out, since I was no longer able to decipher them (Gabelsberger stenography!).

As for polishing the text grammatically (eliminating "And" at the start of sentences and expletives such as "exactly," "precisely," and the like), I was sparing, no doubt more so than Heidegger himself believed necessary for translating these course notes into a book. I considered it no disadvantage if something of his unmistakable style of speaking was preserved in the book. Surely no rendering could convey the rapt fascination which the listeners, so far as they were able to *listen,* experienced when in an utterly unpretentious fashion Heidegger delivered and indeed *read aloud* the text of this course!

Of those who heard the course, no doubt only a few are still living. Among them is my husband, who did not want to share the responsibility of editing this volume. But he was always available to provide counsel and other assistance. I am indebted to his precise scholarly memory for many important points of advice.

Translator's Epilogue

In a peculiar fashion anticipating both the phenomenological hermeneutical analysis of factical Dasein in his 1927 *Being and Time* and the poetic thinking in his later writings after 1930, the theme of Heidegger's lecture course "Ontology—The Hermeneutics of Facticity" from the summer semester of 1923 is succinctly expressed in an inserted page of notes written the following semester (see section III of the Appendix): "Taking our orientation . . . from being and indeed the being-there of Dasein and this concretely as the awhileness of temporal particularity. . . . cf. SS 23 Ontology. . . ." With reference to its title, Heidegger's course is "ontology" because it investigates the "be-ing" (*Sein*) of facticity and more concretely the "be-ing there" (*Dasein*) of factical human Dasein and its world and even more concretely the be-ing there of factical Dasein and its world in the "awhileness of their temporal particularity" (*Jeweiligkeit*). Its theme is the be-ing (factically there for a while at the particular time) of human Dasein and the world. Heidegger's course is at the same time a "logic" or "hermeneutics of facticity" (a phrase to be taken as both an objective and subjective genitive) because it investigates the above theme in the most concrete sense by hermeneutically explicating "at a particular time" (*jeweils*) and in a historical "situation" the "categories" or "existentials" in which factical life, as an open-ended and incalculable "being-possible," "exists (for a while at the particular time)" and "addresses" or "interprets" its be-ing and that of the world. As modes of the be-ing (there), "whiling," and "sojourning" of facticity in the awhileness of its temporal particularity, such existentials are, for example, "temporality," "being in a world," "dealings," "being-interpreted," "talk," the "every-one," "the world's being-encountered," "caring," "spatiality," and the "unpredictable" and "strange." Indeed, Heidegger illustrates such existentials with a long discussion and analysis of "tarrying for a while" in his house and encountering "the table" at which he, his wife, children, and friends pursue their activities (§§19–26). He tells his students that this ontological hermeneutics of facticity is not something being undertaken for the sake of simply "taking cognizance of" and having "knowledge about" facticity, but rather involves an "existential knowing" whose interpretation of the being of facticity is being carried out "with a view to developing in it a radical wakefulness for itself" (p. 12). For the theme of Heidegger's course, see also endnotes 1, 3, and 9 in the Endnotes on the Translation.

In his later work *On the Way to Language*, which reverted to his 1923 course by again using a terminology derived from the poetic verb *weilen* ("to while"), by again speaking of the "sojourning" of human beings, and by again taking up the concept of "hermeneutics" in connection

with Plato's *Ion* 534e ("poets are but the messengers of the gods"),
relating it to "name of the god Ἑρμῆς [Hermes]," the "messenger of
the gods," and defining it as "not just the interpretation but, even before
it, the bringing of a message and announcement [*Kunde*]," Heidegger
said that "Ontology—The Hermeneutics of Facticity" constituted "the
first notes for *Being and Time*."[1] Indeed, the reader will see in its analysis
of "existentials" something of the basic aim and structure of *Being and
Time*, which Heidegger wrote three years later by drawing on his lecture
course manuscripts, though by then the poetic background theme that
such existentials are all characteristics of the "awhileness of the temporal
particularity" of facticity and ways in which it "whiles" had dropped
out and was replaced by the term *Jemeinigkeit*, "mineness" (see §9).
What had also dropped out was Heidegger's powerful fifteen-page phenomenological example of "tarrying for a while" in his home, "being-
in-a-room" there, and the "sewing" of his wife, the "playing" of his
children, his own "writing," and their "daily meals" at the "table" in
this room. This central example was replaced by that of "a hammer,"
and what survived of it was a cursory mention of a "table" in a "room"
with "writing" and "sewing" equipment on it (§15). Insofar as the
underlying theme of "awhileness" and "whiling" in Heidegger's experimental course of 1923 then resurfaced in a different context in his
later writings after 1930, the reader will also see in the analysis of
existentials in this course something of the poetic thinking of Heidegger's later writings (see endnote 9).

In pursuing its innovative ontological hermeneutics of facticity, Heidegger's course lays out the history of hermeneutics from Plato to Dilthey
and briefly takes up from this history the notion that translation is
interpretation (ἑρμηνεία), a kind of hermeneutics. Referring to Aristeas's
account of the translation of the Jewish Pentateuch into Greek in the
third century B.C., Heidegger's course notes read: "τά τῶν Ἰουδαίων
γράμματα ἑρμηνείας προσδεῖται' (the writings of the Jews 'require
translation,' 'interpretation'). Translation: making what was presented in
a *foreign* language accessible in our own language and for the sake of it.
. . . interpreting: pursuing what is authentically meant in a text and
thereby making the matters which are meant accessible, facilitating access to them" (p. 9). The translator is a ἑρμηνεύς ("interpreter"), a term
which Heidegger translates as *Sprecher* ("herald," "spokesman") and
Künder ("messenger"), doing so—as he will later in *On the Way to Language*—in connection with Plato's *Ion* 534e and "the name of the god
Ἑρμῆς [Hermes], the messenger of the gods" (see pp. 6 and 8, as well
as endnote 11). Like the messenger god Ἑρμῆς, the translator is, as a
ἑρμηνεύς, "one who communicates, announces and makes known
[*kundgibt*], to someone what another 'means'" (p. 6). Something of this
ancient notion that translation is interpretation survives today when an

oral translator is called "an interpreter." But what sets Heidegger's approach apart from this convention as well as from most traditional concepts of translation as a branch of hermeneutics is its insistence that a translation is like Hermes the mischievous "messenger of the gods" an interpretive transformation of the message, the translated text. In an essay from 1922 which consisted of Heidegger's translations of Aristotle's basic terms and which the present course drew heavily on, he underscored that "the translation of interpreted texts and above all the translation of their decisive fundamental concepts is something which has grown out of the concrete interpretation of them and contains it, so to speak, *in nuce* [in a nutshell]."[2] Just as translation, a particular kind of hermeneutics, makes a foreign text "accessible in our own language and *for the sake of* it," so generally this Hermes-like "hermeneutics is the announcement and making known [*Kundgabe*] of the being of a being in its being *in relation to . . . (me)*" (p. 7). That translation is interpretation and indeed interpretive transformation became thereafter a life-long theme for Heidegger.[3] In his 1937 foreword to the French translation of his lecture "What Is Metaphysics?" he wrote: "In translation the work of thinking is transposed into the spirit of another language and thus undergoes an inevitable transformation. But the transformation can become fruitful because it makes the fundamental way of posing the question 'what is metaphysics?' appear in a new light."[4] As he elaborated five years later, "a translation can even bring to light connections which indeed exist in the translated language, but have not been made explicit in interpretation. . . . all translation is inevitably interpretation."[5]

Already in this 1923 course he had told his students that the idea of "freedom from standpoints" is an illusion. Our understanding is from the start guided by a factical historical "position of looking" or "point of view" which consists in an interpretive "forehaving" of the object in question (see §16–17 and endnotes 3 and 29). If this forehaving which derives from tradition is rightly appropriated and worked out in our contemporary situation, the object will be "announced and made known" in a new and more appropriate light. It is in light of this that Heidegger says that the task of the Hermes-like translator is that of "making what was presented in a *foreign* language" and in a *foreign* historical period "accessible *in* our own language and *for the sake of* it. . . . pursuing what is authentically meant in a text and thereby making the matters which are meant accessible, facilitating access to them" in "the situation today" (p. 25). Thus he emphasizes that "the forehaving [of interpretation] is not . . . something arbitrary and according to whim" (p. 13), but must be "appropriate" (*entsprechend*) or "fitting" (*angemessen*) to (1) the actuality as well as the untapped and inexplicit possibility of the object and (2) our own "changed historical situation" (pp. 59–60) for approaching it today. In applying this point to the hermeneutics of translation, we can glean

from it two basic hermeneutical standards for the interpretive transfor-
mative work of translation, and it is precisely these standards which the
present translation endeavored to meet.

First, as with any kind of interpretation, the translation of a foreign
text should be fitting to the realities, demands, and limits imposed by
the way the text and its subject matter can and should appear from the
point of view of our own language and historical situation today. In this
sense, a translation should be a translation "of 'its time,'" just as "philosophy is what it can be only as a philosophy of 'its time.' . . . Dasein
works in the how of its *being-now*" (p. 14). In "being-there for a while
at the particular time" in history, a translation should exhibit that characteristic of the "awhileness of temporal particularity" which is usually
easier to see in hindsight, as is the case with, for example, nineteenth-
century translations of Plato or certain translations of Heidegger earlier
in this century which were indeed appropriate for their "particular time"
but have now become anachronistic.

Second, a translation should also be fitting to the actuality and possibilities of the language, conceptuality, and subject matter of the original
text. Heidegger underscores that our interpretive point of view or forehaving must be "explicitly appropriated . . . so that it has been critically
purged" (p. 64). In the case of translation, this forehaving which needs to
be critically appropriated so that it is fitting to the translated text includes
not only the point of view of the translator's own language, but also the
translator's initial philosophical understanding of the meaning of the
translated text and of the intellectual period in the author's development
to which the text belongs. In other words, not only should the original
text undergo a transformation, but so should the language and the thinking of the translator. Each needs to be transformed and accommodated to
the other. A case in point is the need to reproduce, when possible,
Heidegger's many neologisms in the translator's own language. Perhaps
the best example in the present course is the poetic neologism *Jeweiligkeit*,
which could only be accommodated in the English language by correspondingly creating a new word in it, i.e., "awhileness." "Neologisms
employed in translations," Heidegger wrote in 1922, "spring not from an
obsession with innovation, but rather from the content of the translated
texts."[6] Indeed, the creation of an entire idiomatic "Heideggerian language" in philosophical English over the last four or five decades generally
attests to this second hermeneutical standard of translation.

We find both standards applied in Heidegger's own translations of
ancient Greek and Latin texts. Regarding fittingness to the original text,
he told his students that the term λόγος in Aristotle should not be
translated as "reason." ". . . λόγος never means 'reason,' but rather
discourse, conversation—thus man a being which has its world in the
mode of something addressed" (p. 17). And regarding fittingness to our

historical situation and language today, he emphasized that "in a manner appropriate to the changed historical situation, [Aristotle's position] becomes something different and yet remains the same" (p. 60). His innovative translations of the ancient texts of Aristotle and Plato are precisely a Hermes-like attempt to make them come alive and speak again in a new and more fitting way in the German language and "the changed historical situation" of 1923.

So, too, today in the late 1990s this translation of Heidegger's course "Ontology—The Hermeneutics of Facticity" is and attempted to be "something different and yet . . . the same." In my Endnotes on the Translation, I have provided explanations of the linguistic, textual, and philosophical "points of view" which guided my interpretive decisions about how to render the most problematic of Heidegger's terms and passages in a manner which would satisfy the two above-mentioned hermeneutical standards of translation and thus be fitting both to the original text and to our own linguistic situation in the English-speaking world today.[7] I have used endnotes to the body of the translation rather than the Translator's Epilogue for these explanations so that readers can conveniently consult them *in medias res* as they travel along the paths of this difficult and provocative lecture course from Heidegger's youthful period. Endnotes have also been used along with brackets in the body of the text for the quotation of the German text when it is especially problematic.

Translator's endnotes are marked in the translation by bracketed numbers in superscript in order to distinguish them from footnotes, which, except for a few translator's on-page notes marked by symbols, are reproduced from the German edition. Brackets are reserved for my insertions and braces for those within quotations which appear to be Heidegger's, but in some cases could in fact be the editor's. The pagination of the German edition is given between brackets in the running heads.

When Heidegger provides his own innovative translations of Greek and Latin passages and terms and also when he provides no translation (see especially §§2 and 4), I have for the convenience of the reader inserted traditional English translations from published works, though the latter have often been modified somewhat to accommodate Heidegger's interpretation and translation of the foreign text. When published translations were not available, I provided my own. I have followed Heidegger's own heuristic practice in this course of starting with the traditional and (in his view) distorting *interpretive* translations of ancient Greek and Latin texts. His own reason for doing this was that it served as a staging area for a "destruction" or "dismantling" (§15) of these traditional translations, one which endeavored to uncover the founding experiences and meanings in the foreign texts and retrieve them by means of more hermeneutically faithful translations which, in employing devices such as literal renderings, neologisms, and paraphrasing, would allow them to become present again in the historical situation of 1923. The German edition often provides only minimum bibliographical data for foreign and German works cited. I have not undertaken the laborious task of filling out this data in part because such philological lacunae belong to the authentic literary form of Heidegger's text as a set of unpolished course notes.

With reference to the "fundamental questionableness" of hermeneutics, Heidegger states that "the chance that hermeneutics will go wrong belongs in principle to its ownmost being. The kind of evidence found in its explications is fundamentally labile" (p. 12). The interpretations in my translation are no exception. This situation was aggravated by the following especially difficult dimensions of the German text, some of which have also been addressed *in situ* in my endnotes:

Literary form. The text is not a polished book but, as the Editor's Epilogue explains, an incomplete set of often very rough course notes, including marginal comments in the body and "inserts and supplements" in the Appendix. As the editor indicates, the first insert may contain Heidegger's crudely sketched plan for fashioning his course notes into what they certainly are not—a polished "book" (see p. xi and endnote 41). Accordingly, the text was published not in "Division I" of Heidegger's *Collected Edition*, which is reserved for the books and essays he published during his lifetime, but in "Division II: Lecture Courses." In fact, he himself had strong reservations about publishing this and the other sets of course notes from his "early Freiburg period" (1915-23) anywhere in the *Collected Edition*, since it was among other things questionable whether they were or could be put into publishable and readable form.[8] It was not until years after his death that his son and literary executor, Hermann Heidegger, decided to assign them to editors so that they could be deciphered, worked up into publishable form, and included in the *Collected Edition* as a "Supplement" to Division II (see the prospectus for the *Collected Edition* issued by the publisher).

Punctuation. In the body of the text and especially in the Appendix, individual words, phrases, and clauses are sometimes strung together paratactically with a cryptic system of dashes, commas, semicolons, colons, periods, and equal signs—a system sometimes virtually impossible to decipher. The text uses dashes, colons, exclamation marks, and parentheses with more than normal frequency. Sometimes it violates rules of punctuation. One finds a period missing from the end of a sentence, a parenthesis which is not closed, a period appearing mysteriously in the middle of a sentence, uncapitalized words at the start of sentences, and complete sentences beginning with a capital letter and concluding with an end mark which are inserted between parentheses in the middle of other sentences (cf. pp. 25, 35, 52, 62, and 106 in the German edition). I have reproduced most of these cases since they too belong to the authentic literary form of the text as a set of unpolished course notes (cf. pp. 20, 28, 41, 49, and 81ff.).

Sentence structure. While the text contains numerous incomplete sentences, even the complete sentences are often formulated in a highly elliptical and ambiguous way mainly on account of the fact that Heidegger was hastily writing course notes, not preparing a polished book.

Line breaks, indentation, numbered lists, graphics. Especially in certain very rough notes in the Appendix which consist simply of lists of terms, phrases, and fragmentary sentences, one sometimes encounters an unconventional system of line breaks, indentation, and numbered lists which is difficult to decipher. See §§2, 9, 12–14, and 22 in the body and sections I–IV and VIII of the Appendix. At times in the Appendix, line breaks occur after only a few words and without indentation of the following line. At other times, consecutive lines or entire paragraphs are indented. In §21 one also finds a reproduction of Heidegger's enigmatic hand-drawn line which is presumably meant to signal the insertion of text.

Terminology. As documented in the Glossary and in the translator's endnotes, this relatively short text contains over fifty neologisms: for example, *Jeweiligkeit* ("awhileness"), *Je-Verweilen* ("in each case whiling"), *das Da* ("the there"), *Weltdasein-Sein* ("being a worldly being-there"), *das Um* (the "round-about"), *das Zunächst* ("initial givens which are closest to us"), *das man selbst* ("the one-self"), and *das Man* ("the every-one"). There are other aspects of Heidegger's terminology which presented challenges and have accordingly been discussed in endnotes: enigmatic phrases such as *Hinsehen auf Seiendes als Sein* ("looking at beings as be-ing") and *Seiendes vom Sein des faktischen Lebens* ("a being which belongs to the being of factical life") (see pp. 2 and 12); novel philosophical definitions of common terms such as *Fraglichkeit* ("questionableness"), *Destruktion* ("destruction"), *das Heute* ("the today"), *Öffentlichkeit* ("the open space of publicness"), and *Vorschein* ("advance appearance"); use of the original poetic meaning of words such as *Dasein* ("being-there"), *jeweilig* ("in each case for a while at the particular time"), and *Weise* ("pointer," "indicator"); large families of terms formed from root words such as *weilen* ("to while"), *Sein* ("being"), *da* ("there"), *Dasein* ("being-there"), *halten* ("to hold"), *um* ("around," "about"), and *blicken* ("to look"); and cryptic use of the letters "E" and "A" in the first section of the Appendix probably to indicate items in a list, even though the intervening items are not marked with "B," "C," and "D" (see endnote 81).

Many of the above difficulties are also found in Heidegger's other early courses and essays of the late teens and early twenties. They stem to a great extent from the fact that he was at this "particular time" groping uncertainly toward a new beginning in philosophy and experimenting with a new style of thinking and language, one which in the present course included even the novelty of using "the table" in his own home and the play of his "boys" at this table to provide a series of powerful phenomenological illustrations of his often highly abstract philosophical terms. After presenting this to his probably dumbfounded students, Heidegger himself laconically remarked on "the apparent strangeness of the analysis" (p. 73). And regarding his next course in the winter semester of 1923–24 at the University of Marburg, he noted: "'Introduction' Marburg WS 23–24 unsuccessful, usable only if rigorously reworked" (see section III of the Appendix). Indeed, his friend Karl Jaspers later wrote in his autobiography that "Heidegger had already in 1922 read to me a few pages out of a manuscript from that time. It was incomprehensible to me. I pressed for a natural mode of expression."[9] Less than a year before delivering "Ontology—The Hermeneutics of Facticity," Heidegger had been denied a university appointment at the University of Göttingen partly on account of the "tortured character" of his "writing style," as the Dean Georg Misch reported.[10] Another consequence was that he had an article "rejected for publication."[11] Indeed, we find Heidegger himself commenting on the "clumsiness" and "'inelegance' of expression" even in his relatively polished course manuscript from the summer semester of 1925[12] and in his monumental book *Being and Time*.[13] By comparison, "Ontology—The Hermeneutics of Facticity" is, so Heidegger later wrote, only at the primitive level of "the first notes for *Being and Time*."

With the above kinds of difficulties in mind, the editor explains in her epilogue that "as for polishing the text grammatically . . . , I was sparing, no doubt more so than Heidegger himself believed necessary for *translating* [*Umsetzung*] these course notes into a book." She took this approach in her "translating"[14] so that "something of his unmistakable style of speaking was preserved in the book" (p. 90). Following her admirable example[15] of satisfying the two hermeneutical standards of translation outlined above—fittingness to the original text and to the historical situation today—my own "translation" also attempted to retain as much as possible of the unpolished character of the text's original literary form, including the idiosyncratic punctuation, sentence structure, line breaks, indentation, numbered lists, graphics, and terminology which were explained above and which themselves often depart from the basic rules and conventions of the German language, while, on the other hand, it attempted to accommodate the English language in such a way that its present-day rules, conventions, and limits were not excessively strained and Heidegger's text would take on a readable form in English. Like the editor in her work of "translating these course notes into a book," I saw my task to be not that of polishing Heidegger's notes so that they would be easier to read and think about in English than in German, but rather the more Hermes-like one of allowing precisely their probing, unpolished, and at times utterly enigmatic dimensions to speak to us and provoke us again today in a new and fitting way in the "English-speaking" world. As if foreseeing this situation, and with his notion of "formal indication" in mind (see endnote 3), Heidegger wrote in the first section of the Appendix which summarizes the aim of his investigation: "Should be forced by the concrete temporal particularity of the investigation to go back and make an explicit appropriation—true safeguarding against a system and a *polished* philosophy one adopts and opines."

I am grateful to Theodore Kisiel, Thomas Sheehan, and Daniel Dahlstrom for generously reading the manuscript of my translation and offering their sagacious advice on the above-mentioned difficulties in Heidegger's text. I am also grateful to my editors, Janet Rabinowitch, Dee Mortensen, Jeff Ankrom, and Ken Goodall, for their conscientious work and their calm and magnanimity during the flurry of my crucial last-minute revisions. I have the speculative mind and φρόνησις of my wife, Eileen, to thank for helping me to strike a balance between the poetic dimension of Heidegger's text and its factical earthiness. Not having the benefit of a published precedent which could conveniently be consulted on the above-mentioned difficulties, this first English translation of a lecture course from Heidegger's early Freiburg period would not have been possible without the contributions of all the above. Hopefully like the German edition it does its part in proving wrong Heidegger's later suspicion about whether such courses from his early Freiburg period could be put into a readable and worthwhile form.

I dedicate this translation to my beautiful redheaded "co-translator," my daughter, Keely, who made her appearance in the midst of my work and today whiles and plays around our own table.

Notes

1. *Gesamtausgabe*, Vol. 12: *Unterwegs zur Sprache* (Frankfurt: Klostermann, 1985), pp. 19, 10-11, 115, 90; translated as *Poetry, Language, Thought*, trans. Albert Hofstadter (New York: Harper & Row, 1971), pp. 199, 190–92 and *On the Way to Language*, trans. Peter D. Hertz (New York: Harper & Row, 1971), pp. 29, 9 (modified). See also endnote 9 regarding the resurfacing of the terms "whiling" and "sojourning" in Heidegger's later writings.

2. "Phänomenologische Interpretationen zu Aristoteles (Anzeige der hermeneutischen Situation)," *Dilthey Jahrbuch* 6 (1989): 252.

3. For a comprehensive gathering of passages on translation in Heidegger's writings, see Miles Groth, "Heidegger's Philosophy of Translation," Ph.D. dissertation, Fordham University, 1997.

4. *Qu'est-ce que c'est la métaphysique?* trans. Henry Corbin (Paris: Gallimard, 1951), p. 7.

5. *Gesamtausgabe*, Vol. 53: *Hölderlins Hymne "Der Ister"* (Frankfurt: Klostermann, 1984), §12; translated as *Hölderlin's Hymn "The Ister"*, trans. Julia David and William McNeill (Bloomington: Indiana University Press, 1996), §12 (modified).

6. "Phänomenologische Interpretationen zu Aristoteles," p. 242.

7. For a fuller account of the linguistic, textual, and philosophical points of view from which my translation worked, see the discussions of Heidegger's text and its historical context in my book *The Young Heidegger: Rumor of the Hidden King* (Bloomington: Indiana University Press, 1994).

8. See *The Young Heidegger*, p. 15.

9. Karl Jaspers, *Philosophische Autobiographie*, 2d ed. (Munich: R. Piper, 1977), p. 98.

10. "Phänomenologische Interpretationen zu Aristoteles," p. 272.

11. Theodore Kisiel, *The Genesis of Heidegger's Being and Time* (Berkeley: University of California Press, 1993), p. 5.

12. *Gesamtausgabe*, Vol. 20: *Prolegomena zur Geschichte des Zeitbegriffs* (Frankfurt: Klostermann, 1979), pp. 203-4; translated as *History of the Concept of Time: Prolegomena*, trans. Theodore Kisiel (Bloomington: Indiana University Press, 1985), pp. 151-52.

13. *Gesamtausgabe*, Vol. 2: *Sein und Zeit* (Frankfurt: Klostermann, 1977), p. 52; translated as *Being and Time*, trans. John Macquarrie and Edward Robinson (New York: Harper & Row, 1962), p. 63.

14. In his course in the summer semester of 1942, Heidegger explained that translation (*Übersetzung*) also occurs within a single language whenever there is an act of interpretation which restates the original text in a new form and thus "trans-lates" it into this new form: e.g., commentaries on poems and philosophical texts or, as in the present case, deciphering a set of handwritten course notes and editing it into a book). See §12 of *Hölderlins Hymne "Der Ister"*: ". . . all translation is inevitably interpretation. But the converse is also true: all interpretation and everything standing in its service is translation. For translating does not only move between two different languages, but rather there is translating within the same language. An interpretation of Hölderlin's hymns is a translating within our German language." What Heidegger had in mind here was the more literal and general meaning of the German term *Übersetzung* and the Latin term *translatio* (from *transferre*) as "transmission (of a message)," "transference," or "carrying over," a meaning which is still retained in the English term "translation" insofar as we speak of "translating ideas into action" or "translating the past into the present."

15. Theodore Kisiel, who closely compared the German edition with the original manuscript, has reported that he found "only one significant error," which actually turned out to be a "correction" of "Heidegger's own spelling mistake." See Theodore Kisiel, "Edition und Übersetzung: Unterwegs von Tatsachen zu Gedanken, von Werken zu Wegen," in Dietrich Papenfuss and Otto Pöggeler (eds.), *Zur philosophischen Aktualität Heideggers*, Vol. 3: *Im Spiegel der Welt* (Frankfurt: Klostermann, 1992), pp. 93-94.

Endnotes on the Translation

1. "Ontology" was the second of two initial titles Heidegger gave his course. The very first title "Logic" is related to his treatment in §2 of Plato's and Aristotle's characterization of λόγος ("discourse" about being) as ἑρμηνεία ("interpretation") and to his analysis in the same section of the title of Aristotle's Περὶ ἑρμηνείας (*On Interpretation*), where "logic" (study of "discourse" about being) is being characterized as a study of "interpretation," i.e., as hermeneutics. We find this concept of logic as hermeneutics spelled out in Heidegger's important 1922 essay on Aristotle and the "history of ontology and logic." In fact, the treatment of Aristotle, ontology, hermeneutics, facticity, and *Jeweiligkeit* ("the awhileness of temporal particularity," see endnote 9 below) in his course generally draws quite heavily on this essay, and it is cited in n. 4 in §9 (see also endnote 41). See "Phänomenologische Interpretationen zu Aristoteles (Anzeige der hermeneutischen Situation)," *Dilthey Jahrbuch* 6 (1989): 246-47: ". . . philosophy is . . . simply the explicit and genuine actualizing of the tendency to interpretation which belongs to the basic movements of life in which what is at issue is this life itself and its being. . . . The how of its research is the interpretation of the meaning of this being with respect to its basic categorial structures, i.e., the modes in which factical life temporalizes itself and *speaks* (κατηγορεῖν) about itself in such temporalizing. . . . The basic problem of philosophy concerns the *being* of factical life. In this respect, philosophy is *fundamental ontology* and it is this in such a manner that the ontology of facticity provides the particular specialized regional ontologies which are oriented to the world with a foundation for their problems. . . . The basic problem of philosophy has to do with the being of factical life in the how [*jeweiligen Wie*] of its being-addressed and being-interpreted at particular times. In other words, as the ontology of facticity, philosophy is at the same time the interpretation [*Interpretation*] of the categories of this addressing and interpreting [*Auslegen*], i.e., it is *logic*. Ontology and logic need to be brought back to their original unity in the problem of facticity and understood as offshoots of a fundamental kind of research which can be described as the *phenomenological hermeneutics* of facticity."

Thus when Heidegger for external reasons had to replace "Logic" with "Ontology" as the title of his course, he was still thinking of "ontology" (study of the being of facticity in the "awhileness of its temporal particularity") in its unity with "logic" (study of the "categories" or, as Heidegger later in the course also calls them, the "existentials" in terms of which factical life lives and "addresses" its being and that of the world "at particular times") and with a "phenomenological hermeneutics of facticity" (the phenomenological "interpretation" or explication of these categories of "addressing" as categories of "interpreting"). Regarding the theme of Heidegger's course, see also endnotes 3 and 9 and Translator's Epilogue. With this "hermeneutics of facticity" in mind as the most concrete title for the kind of research he was engaged in, Heidegger in the introductory section of his course explained the dangers of describing such research with the traditional and loaded term "ontology" and considered ways of redefining it, but finally at the close of this section replaced "Ontology" with "The Hermeneutics of Facticity" as the course title. Furthermore, in §3 Heidegger went on to explain, as he already had in the above passage from his 1922 essay, that the genitive case in the course title was to be understood both as an objective genitive (i.e., "hermeneutics of facticity" in the sense that hermeneutics has as its thematic object facticity in the "awhileness of its temporal particularity") and as a subjective or possessive genitive ("hermeneutics of facticity" in the sense that such hermeneutics is being carried out by facticity itself as its own "self-interpretation" "at a particular time" and in a historical "situation"). See also Editor's Epilogue for an explanation of the different course titles.

2. *Als Anmerkung zur ersten Anzeige von Faktizität. Nächstgelegene Bezeichnung: Ontologie.* Regarding the problematic German passages quoted in endnotes and between brackets in the body, see the explanation in the Translator's Epilogue of difficulties of sentence structure, punctuation, terminology, line breaks, indentation, numbered lists, and graphics in Heidegger's text which stem from the fact that it is a set of unpolished course notes.

3. "The indefinite and vague directive that, in the following, being should in some thematic way come to be investigated and come to language" translates *die unbestimmte Anweisung . . . , es komme im folgenden in irgendwelcher thematischen Weise das Sein zur Untersuchung und Sprache.* This passage marks the start of Heidegger's introduction of a number of sets of terms to characterize the dynamic intentional-directional and situational sense of "addressing" and "interpreting" the "be-ing (factically there for a while at the particular time)" (*Sein*) of "facticity" in philosophy and in factical life itself (see endnote 5 for the non-objectifying verbal meaning of the term "be-ing," endnote 7 for its connection to *Dasein* ["being-there"], and endnote 9 for its connection to *Jeweiligkeit* ["the awhileness of temporal particularity"]). These sets of terms have been translated as follows:

"Kommen" and its derivatives. As in the above passage, Heidegger uses *kommen* ("to come") and compound verbs formed from it (e.g., *vorkommen* ["to come forth]) for the above-mentioned purpose, and they have accordingly been rendered with "to come" when possible. The phrase *es kommt (ihm) auf . . . an* is at times employed both (1) in its normal meaning of "what is at issue (for it)" or "what it is all about" and (2) in its more literal meaning of "what it all comes to (for it, in it)." In these cases, both above translations have been used when possible. *Zukunft,* which literally means a "coming toward," had to be rendered conventionally as "future." "To come" has also been used in my translation of the neologism *Demnächst* ("initial givens soon to come") which occurs in §18.

Terms formed from "weisen." *Anweisung,* which also occurs in the above passage and derives from *weisen (auf)* ("to point [toward]"), has been translated, along with *Weisung,* as "directive." When in the above passage and elsewhere Heidegger speaks of a "directive," he always means more precisely a directive which directs us "at the particular time," in our historical "situation," and in "our own research" toward and onto the "path" of concretely "researching," "looking at," and "interpreting" the be-ing of facticity in the "awhileness of its temporal particularity." Though in the first part of his course (§6) he uses *Verweis* as a synonym of *Anweisung* and *Weisung,* it and the variant *Verweisung* are rendered as "reference," since later in §11 he assigns *Verweisung* the specific meaning of the "reference" which characterizes the "expressive being" of "temporally particular" cultures and then in sections §§18, 24, and 26 assigns it the even more specific meaning of the "reference" which characterizes the "signifying" and "pointing" (*Be-deuten*) of things which are "there for a while" in everyday life. *Weise* normally means "manner" or "mode" in German, but Heidegger sometimes uses it in its literal meaning of "pointer" or "indicator." In these cases, as in the above passage, I have used "way" as well as "pointing" when possible (cf. endnote 18). Elsewhere, "manner" or "mode" is employed.

Bahn, Weg, Bewegung, Bewegtheit. Weg and *Bahn* have been translated as "path," though "being-on-the-way" has been used for the compound nouns *Unterwegs* and *Unterwegssein.* In connection with these terms, which Heidegger employs to characterize the interpretation of the be-ing of facticity as a "path" or "being-on-the-way," he also describes this interpretation with the terms *Bewegung* or *Bewegtheit* which have been rendered as "motion" and "movement" respectively. Note, however, that in being formed from *Weg* they have the more literal meaning of "being-under-way," which Heidegger himself exploits in §13.

Anzeigen, anzeigend, (formale) Anzeige. Anzeige ("indication"), which has already been introduced in the very first line of Heidegger's course and is a central term in his early writings, is derived from *zeigen* (*auf*), which has the same meaning as *weisen* (*auf*), i.e., "to point (toward)" or "to indicate." Taking this term from the first investigation on "expressions" in Edmund Husserl's *Logical Investigations*, Heidegger uses it and the related terms *Weisung* and *Anweisung* ("directive") to characterize the fundamentally demonstrative, "indicative," or "directive" nature of the concepts he employs insofar as they have the function of "pointing" or "directing" others toward and onto the "concretely existential [*existenziell*]" "path of looking (at)" and interpreting the indicated phenomena of the be-ing of facticity in "[their] own research" (pp. 13, 82). "A *formal indication*," Heidegger writes, "is always misunderstood when it is treated as a fixed universal proposition. . . . Everything depends upon our understanding being guided from out of the indefinite and vague but still intelligible content of the indication onto the right *path of looking*" (p. 62). Accordingly, *Anzeige* is translated as "indication" and "formale Anzeige" as "formal indication." The verb *anzeigen* and the adjective *anzeigend* are rendered as "to indicate" and "indicative" respectively. For Heidegger's use of *Anzeige* as a central term in the early twenties, see my book *The Young Heidegger: Rumor of the Hidden King* (Bloomington: Indiana University Press, 1994), ch. 15 and Theodore Kisiel, *The Genesis of Heidegger's Being and Time* (Berkeley: University of California Press, 1993), pp. 164–70.

"Auf," terms formed from it, and "auslegen." Still another set of terms is formed simply around the preposition *auf* which occurs with a number of the other terms discussed above and below. In some of Heidegger's uses of it, it has all three of its possible directional and horizonal meanings: (1) "toward," (2) "on the basis of" ("starting from"), and (3) "with a view to." In these cases, it is used to describe the following three directional and horizonal dimensions of interpretation: (1) our initial historically influenced and interpretive "position of looking" which already looks *to, toward,* or *with respect to* the being of the object from a definite "point of view" and thus "has" the object "in advance" "as something" in a certain "forehaving" of it; (2) our interpretive "explicating" or "laying out" (*Auslegen*) of the being of the object *on the basis of* this "anticipatory" forehaving and "horizon" insofar as it is a "motivating" and "indicative" "starting point" for a "tendency of

looking" or "path of looking" which needs to be "actualized" (*vollzogen*); and (3) our pursuing this interpretive explication contextually, indicatively, and teleologically *with a view (back) to* (*im Absehen auf*) the underlying context of the being of the object which was initially looked to in (1), so that it can be more fully interpreted within the open-ended "temporalizing" and "being-on-the-way" of interpretation. For the terms "position of looking" (*Blickstand, Blickstellung*) and "point of view" (*Hinsicht*), see endnote 29 and Translator's Epilogue. For the German terms being translated by other English terms in quotation marks above, see the Glossary.

The prime example of the threefold meaning of *auf* is Heidegger's use of this term in the description of his own general "hermeneutics of facticity." In §3, he states that facticity will be "interrogated *auf* the character of its being." As he explains in the same section, this entails the following three moments:

(1) His interpretation initially "engages" facticity and "brings it into play" by looking *to* "the awhileness of the temporal particularity" of its be-ing, i.e., to its "be-ing (factically there as "our own" for a while at the particular time)," and thematizes this be-ing *as* a futural and open-ended "being-possible" or "existence" (see endnote 21) which cannot be "calculated and worked out in advance" as to how it will be "encountered" (see endnote 53), and this is a "position of looking" which, so Heidegger tells us in the Foreword, is historically influenced by Kierkegaard, Luther, and Aristotle.

(2) *On the basis of* this existence as its starting point, the interpretation accordingly will conceptually explicate the various "characteristics" (*Seinscharaktere*), "ways," or "hows" of be-ing (*Wie des Seins*) in the "awhileness of temporal particularity" *as* "categories" or "existentials," i.e., as ways of "being-possible" or "existing" (for a while at the particular time) and as ways of "addressing" or "interpreting" its be-ing (for a while at the particular time) and that of the world. And it will do this by beginning concretely within its own "today" (itself a "defining feature of the awhileness of temporal particularity" and an "existential"), i.e., within the manner in which facticity "today" is "whiling" or "tarrying for a while" in its "present" and in certain "givens which are closest to us" (see endnotes 22 and 35), doing so inauthentically and in a certain condition of "fallenness." It is from out the "today" that other existentials are to be brought to light and explicated. Thus, beginning with an explication of the existential structure of the today, §6 proceeds to give a preliminary list of other existentials found in this setting: "temporality," "being-there," "the there," "being in the world," "being lived from out of the world," "being-interpreted," "publicness," "talk," "averageness," "the every-one," "masking," etc. §§7–13 then focus more concretely on Heidegger's own "today" of 1923 in the form of "historical consciousness today" and "philosophical consciousness today," so that the above existentials and other ones ("having-itself-there," "curiosity," "movement," "falling away," etc.) can be drawn out of it. After a discussion of the method of this phenomenological hermeneutics of facticity (§§14–17), the remainder of the course takes up an even more concrete dimension of Heidegger's own "today" of 1923, i.e., "tarrying for a while at home" in his own household, "being-in-a-room," and encountering "a table" there. In this context, he explicates still other existentials ("whiling," "being in a world," "encountering" the world, "caring," "concern," "going about dealings," "anxious concern," "carefreeness," etc.) as well

as "categories" of the "being-there (for a while at the particular time)" of the world (the "world's being-encountered," "temporality," "kairological moments," "disclosedness," "availability in advance" of what is "ready-to-hand," "significance," the "appearance of the with-world," the "self-world" of the "one-self," "familiarity," the "unpredictable" and "strange," "spatiality," etc.). In an inserted page of fragmentary notes from the following semester, Heidegger returns to the theme of the existential of the "authenticity" of facticity with which he had begun in the introduction to Part One and in §3 and which he had defined as the "worry" and "wakefulness of [facticity] for itself" (for its being-possible and existence). In the insert (see section VI of the Appendix), authenticity is again concretely defined in connection with the "awhileness of the temporal particularity" of facticity as "a genuine *'sojourn'* in which we hold out for a while at the particular time," as "the sojourn *before* the *possibility* of leaping into the work of worried decision." "Sojourning and holding out in life itself. . . . Holding back from a ruinous movement, i.e., being in earnest about the difficulty involved, actualizing the *wakeful* intensification of the difficulty which goes with this. . . ."

(3) As Heidegger also explains in §3, this explication of the existentials of facticity is not being done simply for the sake of "taking cognizance of" and have "knowledge about" facticity, but rather is an "existential knowing" whose interpretation of facticity is being pursued *"with a view [back] to* developing in it a radical wakefulness for itself," i.e., for its authentic existence in the sense of an open-ended *"being-on-the-way* of itself to *itself"* in interpretation. "[Hermeneutics] speaks *from out of* interpretation and for the sake of it." Thus, existence is that *with respect to, on the basis of,* and *with a view to* which the be-ing of facticity in "the awhileness of its temporal particularity" is interpreted in Heidegger's hermeneutics. See endnotes 62 and 75 regarding his use of *auf* when describing "the world" as that "with respect to, on the basis of, and with a view to which" factical life lives and interprets itself inauthentically in "everydayness."

When *auf* and the adverbs *daraufhin* and *daraufzu* have all three of the above meanings, as they often do when used in conjunction with *befragen* ("to interrogate") and *auslegen* ("to interpret"), I have used "with respect to, on the basis of, and with a view to" for them. In other cases where *auf* occurs as a technical term, I use either "with respect to," "on the basis of," "toward," "in the direction of," "to," "at," or some combination of these. For example, *aussein auf* is rendered as "to be out for and going toward." "With respect to" has been reserved for *auf,* since it comes closest to expressing the threefold meaning of this German term. When *auf* in the sense of "on the basis of" is used in conjunction with *auslegen* ("to interpret [on the basis of]"), the reader should keep in mind the literal directional meaning of *auslegen* as "laying *out.*" Accordingly, Heidegger employs *Explizieren* ("explicating"), *Explikation* ("explication"), and *Ausbildung* ("development," "working out") as virtual synonyms of *Auslegung* ("interpretation"). "Interpreting," "interpretation," "being-interpreted" ("having-been-interpreted"), and "to interpret" have been used respectively for *Auslegen, Auslegung, Ausgelegtheit,* and *auslegen,* though in a few cases *auslegen* is rendered as "to explicate interpretively."

The most interesting of Heidegger's terms which are formed from *auf* is the neologism *Woraufhin,* even though it occurs only once in §7. Heidegger borrowed it and the more frequently used variant *Worauf* from his 1922 essay on Aristotle in which they figured as central terms. See "Phänomenologische Interpretationen zu Aristoteles," pp. 237ff. *Woraufhin* also became a central term in Heidegger's *Being and Time*, and the English translators of this work have rendered it as "the 'upon-which'." See *Gesamtausgabe*, Vol. 2: *Sein und Zeit* (Frankfurt: Klostermann, 1977), p. 201; translated as *Being and Time*, trans. John Macquarrie and Edward Robinson (New York: Harper & Row, 1962), pp. 193ff. I have used the fuller translation "the with-respect-to-which and on-the-basis-of-which" since the German term means the initial situational and interpretive forehaving of the being of the object "with respect *to* which" and "*on* the basis of which" the object is explicated. The related neologism *Worauf* is translated either as "the toward-which" or as "the whereto."

Intentional terms appropriated from Husserl. Not only does Heidegger's discussion of Husserl's phenomenology occupy a central place in his course (§14), but his characterization of the dynamic directional nature of the interpretation of the be-ing of facticity takes up, though with less emphasis than in his preceding writings, the following four terms which Husserl had used to describe different aspects of the intentionality of consciousness, i.e., of its "being-directed toward" (*Gerichtetsein auf*) something: (1) *Bezogensein auf . . .* (interpretation's "being-related to . . ." at the particular time), *Bezug auf* ("relation to [toward] . . ."), or *Sichverhalten zu* ("comporting-itself toward . . ."); (2) the *Gehalt* ("content") to which interpretation is directed and related, i.e., the being of the object; (3) the *Vollzug* ("actualizing") of the interpretive relation to . . . ; and (4) the ongoing *Zeitigung* ("temporalizing and unfolding") of this actualizing of the interpretive relation to. . . . Regarding *Zeitigung* and *Vollzug*, see also endnote 26.

Terms formed from "richten." Closely connected with this last set of terms is another which consists of *richten (auf)* ("to direct [toward]") and other terms formed from it: *Gerichtetsein auf* ("being-directed toward"), *Verrichten* ("directing ourselves to tasks"), *Richtung auf* ("direction toward"), *Auslegungsrichtung* ("direction of interpretation"), and *Blickrichtung auf* ("direction of looking toward"). In connection with these terms, the above Husserlian intentional terms, and the phrase *auslegen auf* ("to interpret with respect to and on the basis of"), Heidegger uses a pair of terms consisting of *Tendenz* (the "tendency" of interpretation, what it "tends" toward) and *Motiv* (the "motive," what "motivates" the tendency or direction of interpretation, i.e., the initial historically influenced "position of looking" and its "with-respect-to-which and on-the-basis-of-which").

4. See Translator's Epilogue for an explanation of brackets and braces.

5. *Gerade nicht auf das Sein als solches, d.h. das gegenstandsfreie.* The German noun *Sein* is formed directly from the infinitive *sein* ("to be") and thus has an even stronger verbal sense than the English gerund "being." In contrasting it with the static concept of "object" throughout his course, describing it as an "unpredictable" and "incalculable" *Begegnen* ("being-encountered," "happening," see endnote 53), and using it in conjunction with the literal poetic and situational meanings of the terms *Dasein* ("being-there") and *Jeweiligkeit* ("the awhileness of temporal particularity"), Heidegger intends *Sein* to be understood in the dynamic and non-objectifying verbal, directional, situational, and thus demonstrative or "indicative" sense of "be-ing," i.e., of the "be-ing (there for a while at the particular time)" of facticity. This is the case not only when he is discussing the situational be-ing or "signifying (for a while)" of things in everyday life such as the table, books, and skis in his

home (§§19–20), but especially when he is addressing the "existential" (*existenziell*) be-ing of "our own" lives (subjective and objective genitive), where the concept of "object" is particularly inappropriate. Even though the unhyphenated term "being" is, with a few exceptions, subsequently used for *Sein*, the reader should in the vast majority of cases hear in it the strong verbal meaning of the hyphenated term "be-ing." The same applies to Heidegger's numerous compound terms which include *Sein* and are for the most part neologisms: for example, *seinsmäßig* ("in the manner of be-ing"), *Seinscharakter* ("character[istic] of being"), *Dasein* ("being-there"), *Wachsein* ("being-wakeful," "wakefulness"), and *Sein in einer Welt* ("being in a world"). See the Glossary for other compound terms. The convention of using the capitalized noun "Being" for *Sein* has been jettisoned in order to ward off any suggestion of the reifying, objectifying, generalizing, essentializing, and deperson-alizing of "be-ing" against which this course so emphatically argues. *Seiendes*, which also often has a strong verbal sense for Heidegger, has been rendered as "beings" or "a being." Note that later in the present section Heidegger says that his herme-neutical ontology involves "looking at beings as be-ing [*Seiendes als Sein*]." Thus as with "being," the reader should hear in the unhyphenated terms "beings" and "a being" the strong verbal meaning of the hyphenated terms "be-ings" and "a be-ing." In a few cases in which it is unclear whether *Sein* or *Seiendes* is being translated, the German term has been inserted between brackets.

6. "Mean-ing" translates *Meinen*. See endnote 59.

7. The German phrase is *nicht aber aus Dasein*. The philosophical term *Dasein* means "being," "existence," or more specifically "human existence," though its literal demonstrative or "indicative" meaning on which Heidegger's poetic use of this term draws in conjunction with the terms "facticity," "be-ing," and the "awhileness of temporal particularity" is "being-there," i.e., "be-ing (factically) there (for a while at the particular time)." I follow the custom of leaving it for the most part untranslated and using "being-there" when Heidegger puts special emphasis on its literal meaning, as he does especially in the last two chapters of the text, where he deals with the "being-there" of both the world and human life (see endnote 56). Even when it is translated simply as "Dasein," the reader should keep in mind the literal meaning of "being-there" on which Heidegger is constantly and poetically drawing. In cases where it refers specifically to human life and thus has the "existential" sense of the "be-ing there" of "our own" lives, sometimes "Dasein" and "being-there" have been employed together in the phrases "the being-there of Dasein" and "Dasein in its being-there," which re-spectively have the sense of "the being-there of human life" and "human life in its being-there." In the present passage, where it is unclear whether "Dasein" refers to the "being-there" of the world or to that of human being, the phrase "[the world's] being-there for Dasein" has been used. The above phrases are no more redundant than a similar mode of expression which Heidegger uses in the German text: *Dasein ist da . . .* ("Dasein [being-there] is there . . ."). The German term has been inserted between brackets when Heidegger hyphenates *Dasein* in order to call special attention to its literal meaning.

Heidegger also uses a number of neologisms which are formed either from the noun *Dasein*, from the verb *dasein* ("to be there"), or simply from the adverb *da* ("there"). These include *dabeisein* ("to be at home there," "be involved in"), *Da-bei-sein* ("being-there-at-home-in," "being-there-involved-in"), *Daseiendes* ("beings-which-are-there," "those-who-are-there"), *Mitdaseiendes* ("those-who-are-there-with-us"), *Weltdasein-Sein* ("being a worldly being-there"), *Immerdasein* ("always-being-there"), *Dingdasein* ("being-there of things"), *So-da-sein* ("being-there-in-such-and-such-a-manner"), *Zu-handen-da-sein* ("being-there-ready-to-hand"), *Da-zu-sein* ("being-there-in-order-to-do-this"), *Dazu* ("there-in-order-to-do-this"), *Da-für-dasein* ("being-there-for-this"), *Dafür* ("there-for-this"), *Sich-selbstdahaben* ("having-itself-there"), *das Da* ("the there"), and *Da-Charakter* ("the character of the there").

Regarding the connection between the spatial meaning of *Dasein* as "being-there," the term *Öffentlichkeit* ("the open space of publicness") in §6, and the theme of "factical spatiality" in §§18 and 26, see endnotes 34, 62, and 75.

8. "One" and "everyone" have been reserved for translating the pronoun *man*. See endnote 36.

9. *Genauer bedeutet der Ausdruck:* jeweilig *dieses Dasein (Phänomen der "Jeweiligkeit"; cf. Verweilen, Nichtweglaufen, Da-bei-, Da-sein), sofern es* seinsmäßig *in seinem Seinscharakter* "da" *ist.* This sentence contains a number of "indicative" German terms which derive from the poetic verb *weilen* ("to while"), occur frequently as technical terms, and are used in close connection with "be-ing," "being-there (for a while at the particular time)," and another group of poetic terms formed from *halten*. These terms and those formed from *halten* have been translated as follows:

Jeweiligkeit, Verweilen, Weile. The neologism *Jeweiligkeit* is coined from the adjective *jeweilig*, which normally means "respective," "prevailing," or "at the particular time" (cf. *der jeweilige König* ["the king at the particular time"]), but has the literal meaning of "in each case [*je*] for a while at the particular time [*weilig*]." Accordingly, in coining the term *Jeweiligkeit*, Heidegger has in mind both its more conventional meaning of something like "temporal particularity" and its literal meaning of "awhileness," i.e., the characteristic of "whiling" or "tarrying for a while" (*Verweilen*) in the "there" of "being-there" and along a finite "span" of temporality (see especially §§18ff.). This literal meaning comes to the fore especially when Heidegger later in §20 poignantly illustrates it with the things, people, and activities which have been or are "there" "for a while" in his own home. *Jeweiligkeit* has therefore been translated mostly in a compound form as "the awhileness of temporal particularity" and sometimes simply as "awhileness." In Heidegger's course, the *Jeweiligkeit* of the be-ing (there) of facticity and, more concretely, of the be-ing (there) of human beings and the world refers to at least three dimensions: (1) the *particularity* or *individuality* of their "be-ing there," (2) their "be-ing there" or "whiling (there)" *at the particular time,* and (3) their "be-ing there" or "tarrying (there)" *for a while.* Indeed, the intimate connection between the themes of "be-ing," "being-there," and the "awhileness of temporal particularity" is clearly indicated by Heidegger in his summarizing notes on his course. See section I of the Appendix: "*Themes:* A. Facticity—ontology—being—the awhileness of temporal particularity—Dasein in its being-there: each related to hermeneutics." See also section III which bears the title "Overview": "Taking our orientation . . . from being and indeed the being-there of Dasein and this concretely as the awhileness of temporal particularity, today. (cf. SS 23 Ontology.)"

In order to maintain its relation to *Jeweiligkeit*, the gerund *Verweilen (bei)* has, depending on context, been translated either with both "whiling (at home in)" and "tarrying for a while (awhile)" or with one of the following: "tarrying for a while (awhile)," "tarrying (among)," "tarrying-for-a-while," "tarrying-awhile." The enigmatic neologism *Je-Verweilen* in §6 has been rendered as "in each case whiling, tarrying for a while." "Its while" has been employed for the single occurrence of the substantive noun *seine Weile* in §18.

Jeweilig, jeweils, jeweilen, je. The adjectival and adverbial terms *jeweilig, jeweils*, and *jeweilen* have been translated mainly with "in each case for a while at the particular time" or with some component of this phrase. Heidegger usually uses them as technical terms and accordingly often uses *jeweilig* in an unconventional manner as an adverb and revives the archaic adverb *jeweilen*. See the Glossary for other less frequent renderings of the above German terms especially when Heidegger employs them also in conventional ways. When some form of "while" was not able to be used, as in those cases of employing "temporally particular" or simply "particular" for *jeweilig*, the German term has in relevant cases been inserted between brackets or in an endnote so that the reader can keep in mind the reference to "while" in its literal meaning. Even when "while" was used, the German text has been provided when a difficult translation decision had to be made. The adjective "particular" has been reserved for the above usages and has not been employed for *bestimmt*, which, though conventionally rendered as "particular," has rather been translated for the most part as "definite" in order to maintain its relation to *bestimmen* ("to define"), *Bestimmung* ("definition"), *Bestimmtheit* ("definiteness"), and *unbestimmt* ("indefinite [and vague]"). When *je* occurs by itself as an adverb, "in each case" has for the most part been used.

See endnotes 22 and 34 regarding the theme that the being-there of Dasein is a "whiling" in "the today" (*Heute*), "the present" (*Gegenwart*), "presence" (*Präsenz*), and "the open space of publicness" (*Öffentlichkeit*), endnote 26 regarding the connection between "whiling" and "temporalizing" (*Zeitigung*), and endnotes 62 and 75 regarding the theme introduced in §6 and explored in §§18ff. that the "disclosedness" and "being-interpreted" of "the there" of "the world" and its "factical spatiality" are that wherein Dasein as "being in a world" "whiles."

Connected terms formed from "halten." Heidegger uses another group of poetic terms in connection with those above, i.e., (*sich*) *halten, sich aufhalten, Aufhalten* (*bei*), *Aufenthalt*, and other terms formed from *halten*. The verb *sich halten auf* means literally "to halt" or "hold oneself" (*sich halten*) "at" (*auf*) some place, linger there, and "not run away," as Heidegger colloquially puts it in the passage with which this endnote began. Thus two common meanings of *sich halten* on which Heidegger draws are (1) "to last," "keep," or "hold out" and (2) "linger," "stay," or "hang around." It and the above terms formed from it are clearly connected to Heidegger's characterization of the "being-there of Dasein" as a "having-itself-there" (*Sich-da-haben*) and "whiling" in this "there" (pp. 40ff.). For example, in his treatment of "historical consciousness" in Oswald Spengler and others, Heidegger discusses the theme of the unified "style" in which a culture "comes to expression, holding itself therein, lingering for a time, and then becoming anti-quated [*darin sich hält und veraltet*]" (§7). He also uses *sich halten* in §§11–12 to speak of the way that contemporary historical consciousness and philosophy "hold themselves" and "linger" in their "there," i.e., in their "present" (*Gegenwart*) or "today" (*Heute*) which is co-defined by the "open space of publicness" (*Öffentlichkeit*). And just as he speaks of the "be-ing," "being-there," and "whiling" not only of human beings but also of things such as the "table" in his home, so he also says that in everydayness a thing such as a table *"holds itself* [hält sich] in [its] being-there and being-available, *lingering* in them in accord with the awhileness of temporal particularity in question and throughout it" (§21).

Accordingly, *sich halten* is translated with "to hold (itself)" and "to linger," *sich aufhalten* with "to hold itself and sojourn," *Aufhalten (bei)* with "sojourning (at home in)," "holding itself (in)", and "holding out (in)," and *Aufenthalt* with "sojourn," "abode," "holding out," and "halting." Especially in connection with Heidegger's key phenomenological example of "tarrying for a while at home" and "being-in-a-room" there (§§19ff.), the reader should keep in mind other possible and more homey translations of *sich aufhalten* ("dwell," "abide," "reside") and of *Aufenthalt* ("dwelling place," "residence," "home"). Whenever possible, "to hold" has also been employed in translating the large number of other terms formed from *halten: behalten* ("to hold onto," "preserve"), *erhalten* ("to gain a foothold," "preserve," "hold open"), *festhalten* ("to hold fast [to]"), *aushalten* ("to hold out"), *durchhalten* ("to hold out until the end"), *vorhalten* ("to hold up before"), *halten an* ("to require to hold to"), *Behaltbarkeit* ("ability of preservation [of the past] to hold onto it"), *Im-Blick-halten* ("holding-in-view"), *Sichverhalten (zu)* ("comporting-itself [toward]," "self-comportment," "comportment [toward]," "holding-itself in the comportment"), *Verhalten* ("comporting," "comportment"), *Halt* ("a hold"), *Haltung* ("stance held to"), *aufenthaltslos* ("abode-less," "never halting, making a sojourn, and holding out there"), *Enthalten* ("holding back").

Bei. As the passage at the start of this endnote makes clear, the preposition *bei* which is used with *verweilen* and *aufhalten* has the meaning of "at" or "in" in the sense of "being-there-*at-home-in*" and "being-there-*involved-in*" (*Da-bei-sein*). Its meaning is thus close to that of the French *chez* ("at [someone's home, place, etc.])." In *Being and Time* Heidegger explains that its original etymological meaning is that of *"sich aufhalten bei"* ("to sojourn at home in"). See *Sein und Zeit*, p. 73; *Being and Time*, p. 80. In their translation of *Being and Time*, Macquarrie and Robinson use "alongside" for *bei*, but since this suggests a sense of detachment which is foreign to what Heidegger has in mind, I have not used it. When *bei* occurs as a technical term with the meaning explained above, it is rendered as "in," "at home in," or "among."

When the introduction to Part One, §6, and §§18ff. of Heidegger's course explore the "there" of Dasein and its world as that wherein it "whiles," when §§24 and 26 explain that the ἀλήθεια ("truth," "uncoveredness," "disclosedness") of the "there" of the world is that "wherein concern holds itself and sojourns [*sich aufhält*]" insofar as this concern is a "ἕξις" ("state of having," "habit") or *Gewohnheit* ("habitual way of dwelling," "habit," "custom"), when §§11-12 refer to the interpretation of being in historical consciousness and philosophy as an *Aufenthalt* ("sojourn," "abode"), *Halt* ("hold"), *Da* ("there"), and *Ort* ("place"), and when sections V and VI of the Appendix state that "philosophy . . . is only a definite kind of sojourning at home in . . . [*Aufhalten bei-*]," muse on the "Greek sojourn [*Aufenthalt*] and its doctrine of being," and argue that philosophy is "able to see *movement* in an authentic manner only from out of a genuine *'sojourn'* ['Aufenthalt'] in which we hold out for a while at the particular time," all this is similar to terminology in Heidegger's later writings after 1930. Here Heidegger again says, though in a different context, that ontology thinks about being as the "sojourn" or "abode [*Aufenthalt*] of human beings." As he explains, ontology can thus be called an "original ethics" since the term ἦθος from which "ethics" is formed means not just that Aristotelian concept of "moral character" in the sense of ἕξις ("state of having," "habit") or *Gewohnheit* ("habitual way of dwelling," "habit") which he had dealt with in his earlier reading of Aristotle's ethics in his 1923 course (see also endnote 29), but also literally "home" in the sense of the kind of "abode" or "sojourn" which he had also hinted at in his 1923 course. See "Brief über den Humanismus," in *Gesamtausgabe*, Vol. 9: *Wegmarken* (Frankfurt: Kostermann, 1976), p. 356; translated as "Letter on Humanism," trans. Frank A. Capuzzi, in *Pathmarks*, ed. Wllliam McNeill (Cambridge: Cambridge University Press, 1998), p. 271 (modified). Was the course "Ontology—The Hermeneutics of Facticity" the original form of Heidegger's "original ethics"? The innovative poetic terminology which he fashioned from the verbs *halten* ("to hold") and *weilen* ("to while") in order to muse on the "sojourning" and "whiling" of the be-ing (there) of facticity in this experimental lecture course receded into the background in his subsequent writings of the twenties and only came to the fore again in the different context of his later writings. For Heidegger's later use of *weilen* and other terms formed from it, cf. the following works: *Der Satz vom Grund* (Pfullingen: Neske, 1957); translated as *The Principle of Reason*, trans. Reginald Lilly (Bloomington: Indiana University Press, 1991). "*Der Spruch des Anaximander,*" in *Gesamtausgabe*, Vol. 5: *Holzwege* (Frankfurt: Kostermann, 1977), pp. 321–73; translated as "The Anaximander Fragment," in *Early Greek Thinking*, trans. David Farrell Krell and Frank A. Capuzzi (New York: Harper & Row, 1975), pp. 13–58. See also Translator's Epilogue.

10. Regarding "to open up" (*öffnen*) and "to circumscribe" (*umgrenzen*), see endnotes 34 and 75.

11. Both "to announce" and "to make known" have been used here to translate *kundgeben*, which is the term Heidegger employs to describe what ἑρμηνεύειν ("interpreting") precisely does. Both English terms are used since neither by itself expresses the twofold meaning of *kundgeben*: (1) its linguistic and kerygmatic meaning of "to announce," "proclaim," "herald," "communicate," or "express" and (2) its phenomenological meaning of "to reveal" or "make known." In connection with Heidegger's earlier reference to the etymological connection between "hermeneutics" and "Hermes" (the "messenger of the gods"), his translation of Plato's *Ion* 534e ("poets are but the interpreters of the gods" in the sense of their "heralds" [*Sprecher*]), his later translation of Philo's phrase ἑρμηνεὺς θεοῦ ("interpreter of God," a description of Moses) as "messenger who announces [*Künder*] . . . the will of God," and his later discussion of Augustine's Christian hermeneutics as the kerygmatic interpretation of the Word, note that *Kunde* means "message," "news," or "tidings" and that accordingly *kundgeben* (the activity of hermeneutics, interpretation) means literally "to give news (tidings)" or "bring a message." It is against this background that Heidegger writes in the following paragraph in connection with ontology, the study of being: "hermeneutics is the announcement and making known [*Kundgabe*] of the being of a being in its being in relation to . . . (me)." He then proceeds to relate this kerygmatic dimension of hermeneutical ontology to its more phenomenological dimension by appealing to Aristotle's *On Interpretation* and defining "interpretation" as "ἀληθεύειν [being-true] (making what was previously concealed, covered up, available as unconcealed, as there out in the open)."

Even though "to make known" will henceforth mostly be used for *kundgeben*, the reader should constantly keep in mind both the kerygmatic and the phenomenological meanings of the German term. Regarding Heidegger's kerygmatic reading of "hermeneutics" and "ontology," on which he continues to draw in his later writings, see also Translator's Epilogue.

12. Regarding "going about dealings" (*Umgang*), see endnote 75.

13. The unconventional format of the numbered lists in the German edition has been reproduced.

14. *Die Auslegung is Seiendes vom Sein des faktischen Lebens selbst.*

15. "Interrogated with respect to and on the basis of" translates *befragt auf.* See endnote 3.

16. The single previous occurrence of *Einsatz* was translated simply as "engaging," but here "initially engaging and bringing into play" has been used. Subsequently, *Einsatz* is rendered as "initial engagement and bringing into play" and the verb *einsetzen* as "to engage itself (and bring itself into play)" or as "to put forth initially and bring into play." *Einsatz*, which Heidegger always uses in the sense of "the initial (interpretive) engaging and bringing into play (of the be-ing of facticity)," has a rich array of meanings on which he draws in connection with the theme of the dynamic directional sense of interpretation discussed in endnote 3: (1) the philosophical meaning of "starting point" in our "approach" to and "engagement" of subject matter; (2) the musical and theatrical meaning of the "entrance" of the orchestra or the "coming in" (of the violins, etc.); (3) the military meaning of "engagement," "deployment," or "bringing into action" of troops; (4) the game-related meaning of "bringing (a chess piece, ball, etc.) into play"; and (5) the aleatory meaning of "risk" or "stake." With these meanings in mind, as well as his theme that philosophy is a "mode of Dasein's self-encounter" (see endnote 53) and of its "wakefulness" for itself, Heidegger states in the very next paragraph that the "initial engagement and bringing into play" of facticity hermeneutically "transports" (*versetzt*) it into an experience and interpretation of itself "in the moment." Note also his explicit appeal to the above-mentioned game-related and aleatory meanings later in this section when he describes "the initial hermeneutical engagement and bringing into play" of facticity as "that with respect to, on the basis of, and with a view to which everything is like a card in a game staked." The verb *ergreifen* is sometimes used in connection with *Einsatz* as well as *Wachsein* ("wakefulness") and here means not only "to grasp" or "understand" facticity, but also "to seize," "stir," "rouse," or "move" it. In these cases, it has been translated as "to grasp and stir." *Ansatz*, which Heidegger uses in conjunction with *Einsatz*, has been rendered as "starting point" and "(initial) approach."

17. Heidegger had been using the homey but clumsy technical term *Bekümmerung* ("worry") since around 1920. See "Anmerkungen an Karl Jaspers *Psychologie der Weltanschauungen*," in *Wegmarken*, pp. 5ff.; translated as "Comments on Karl Jaspers's *Psychology of Worldviews*," trans. John van Buren, in *Pathmarks*, pp. 4ff. This term is most clearly defined in Heidegger's 1922 essay on Aristotle: "Worry refers not to a mood in which we wear a woebegone expression, but rather to a factical being-resolved, i.e., seizing upon our *existence* . . . as something we are and will be concerned about. . . . worry is the care of existence (*gen. ob.* [objective genitive])." See "Phänomenologische Interpretationen zu Aristoteles,"

p. 243. In the present section of Heidegger's course, *Bekümmerung* is used not only in connection with Dasein's "caring" (*Sorgen*) about itself (i.e., about its "existence" or "possibility") and with its "unrest" (*Unruhe*), but also in connection with its "wakefulness for itself," a phrase which occurs in the preceding paragraph and is in §26 contrasted to the "carefreeness" in which "care is asleep." However, in this course Heidegger is already in the process of replacing *Bekümmerung* with the perhaps less clumsy and more sophisticated Kierkegaardian term *Angst* ("anxiety" or "anxiousness"), which eventually becomes a central term in *Being and Time*. *Bekümmerung* and the adjective *bekümmert* (see section VI of the Appendix) each occur only once in this course and are translated as "worry" and "worried" respectively. Other possible translations of *Bekümmerung* include "being troubled," "being disturbed," "concern," "distress," and "anxiousness." However, "anxious" has been reserved for translating *Besorgnis*, an intensive form of *Besorgen* ("concern," "being concerned about and attending to") which Heidegger uses in §§21 and 26 to describe Dasein's being "anxiously concerned" or "worried" about itself in a "worldly" manner. *Besorgnis* has accordingly been rendered not just as "concern," which for Heidegger means concern about the world, but more strongly as "anxious concern and its apprehensions," since this rendition suggests the "intensity" (p. 72) of concern and the involvement of the self which Heidegger intends. Note that the etymological connection between *Besorgen* and *Besorgnis*, on the one hand, and *Sorgen* and *Sorge*, on the other, is lost in my respective translations of the latter terms as "caring" and "care." "To distress" and "to disturb" were reserved for translating *Bedrängnis* ("distress," "something distressing"), *stören* ("to disturb"), and *Störbarkeit* ("disturbability"), terms which Heidegger employs in §§25–26 to describe the "awakening" of the "carefreeness" in which "care is asleep." Regarding "anxious concern and its apprehensions," "concern," and "care," see also endnotes 62 and 75.

18. *Grundbegriffe sind keine Nachträglichkeiten, sondern vor-tragend: Dasein in den Griff nehmen in ihrer Weise.* See endnote 3 on *Weise*, which in the above sentence has been rendered as "way of pointing."

19. *Grundfraglichkeit in der Hermeneutik and ihres Absehens: Der Gegenstand: Dasein ist nur in ihm* selbst. The term *Fraglichkeit* which occurs in this grammatically idiosyncratic sentence as well as elsewhere has been rendered as "questionableness." Retaining overtones of its normal meaning of "doubtfulness" or "uncertainty," *Fraglichkeit* means for Heidegger something like "being able to be questioned," "open to question," or "disputable." Note his statement earlier in the present section that "the kind of evidence found in [hermeneutics] is fundamentally labile" and thus open to question.

20. *Diese ist reluzent in alle Seinscharaktere; ontische Fraglichkeit: Sorgen, Unruhe, Angst, Zeitlichkeit.*

21. *(Fraglich haben, wie Anlageproblem und ob überhaupt zu stellen. Wird nicht von der Fraglichkeit das* Möglichsein *sichtbar als eigenständig konkret existenziell?)* The three occurrences of *existenziell* in the present section and in section VI of the Appendix have been translated as "existential." In its common spelling, i.e., *existentiell*, this term has the same meaning as the present-day English term "existential" in usages such as "of existential significance." Heidegger indeed intends *existenziell* to be understood in this common meaning, but he defines it—in connection with the Kierkegaardian term *Existenz* ("existence") introduced earlier in this section

(see also endnote 3)—more precisely as referring to the "*ownmost* possibility of be-ing" "my own" factical life in the "awhileness of its temporal particularity" in contrast to an external and reifying approach to human life as an "object" of knowledge. Heidegger later in §4 of *Being and Time* contrasts *existenziell* with *existenzial* (Macquarrie and Robinson use "existentiell" and "existential" respectively for these terms), explaining that the former refers to "existing itself" in its concrete "mineness" (*Jemeinigkeit*) and the latter to the "structures of existence" explicated in hermeneutical ontology. But in the present text he does not make this terminological distinction. The term *existenzial* is not used anywhere. However, Heidegger does, as in *Being and Time*, employ the noun *Existenzialien* ("existentials") to designate the always temporally particular "categories" or "structures" of "existing (for a while at the particular time)" and "interpreting" which hermeneutical ontology explicates and expresses in "formal indications." The term *ontisch* ("ontic") occurs in the previous paragraph and in §7. *Ontologisch* ("ontological") occurs throughout the course. These terms appear to have the same meaning that they do later in §4 of *Being and Time*, where "ontic" refers to "beings" and their actual "be-ing" (or, in the case of human beings, their actual "existing") and "ontological" refers to the categories or structures of the "being" of these beings which are explicated in ontology. Note that "existence" and "existential" have been reserved for *Existenz* and *existenziell* since Heidegger assigns these terms the very specific meanings explained above.

22. *Das Heute* ("the today") is reintroduced and explained in §§6 and 10 as a "defining feature of the awhileness of temporal particularity," i.e., "the today" or "the world today" is something wherein the being-there of Dasein "whiles" (see also endnote 3). *Das Heute* is the nominal form of the adverb *heute* ("today") and accordingly has the conventional meaning of "these days" or "the present times." However, since Heidegger uses it in its literal meaning as a key technical term, I have rendered it literally as "the today," following Macquarrie's and Robinson's practice in their translation of *Being and Time*. The adverb *heute* and the adjective *heutig* have been rendered as "today" or "today's." "The present" and "presence" have been reserved respectively for *Gegenwart* and *Präsenz*, terms which Heidegger uses in conjunction with *Heute* when he speaks of Dasein "lingering" or "whiling" in "the present" and "presence" (see §§6, 13, and 16). Terms related to *Gegenwart* have been translated as follows: *gegenwärtig* ("present"), *vergegenwärtigen* ("to make present," "to present"), *Vergegenwärtigung* ("presenting," "presentation"). Those related to *Präsenz* have been translated as follows: *präsent* ("[made] present"), *Präsenthaben* ("having-present"), *Präsentsein* ("being-present"), *Selbstpräsentation* ("self-presentation"). Since Heidegger intends *präsentieren* in both its literal temporal meaning of "to make present (in the today)" and its more conventional meaning of "to present" or "introduce (in the public realm)," it has usually been rendered as "to make present and put forward (offer, introduce)." *Repräsentieren* has been rendered as both "to make present" and "to represent."

23. "The '*every-one*'" translates *das* Man. See endnote 36.

24. "Is encountering" translates *begegnet*. See endnote 53.

25. The German phrase is *jeweilig bestimmte historische* Möglichkeit.

26. "To temporalize and unfold" translates the term *zeitigen* which occurs again in §18. *Zeitigung*, which occurs in §26 and in section V of the Appendix, is

rendered as either "temporalizing" or "temporalization." These terms are related to *Zeit* ("time") and *Zeitlichkeit* ("temporality") and even more closely to *zeitig* ("timely," "seasonable," "ripe," "mature," "having unfolded"). Heidegger accordingly intends *zeitigen* both in its philosophical meaning of "to temporalize" and in its common meaning of "to unfold, ripen, and bear fruit (in season, at the right time)," as when one speaks of the "ripening" (*Zeitigung*) of grapes "in season." Having this reference to what is "timely" or "in season," the meaning of *zeitigen* is connected to that of *verweilen* ("to tarry for a while at the particular time"). As is made clear by Heidegger's 1922 essay on Aristotle and by his translation of a passage from Aristotle's *De anima* in §2 of the present text, he uses the term *Vollzug* which occurs in conjunction with *Zeitigung* to translate Aristotle's term ἐνέργεια ("actuality"), and it has accordingly been rendered as "actualizing" or "actualization." See "Phänomenologische Interpretationen zu Aristoteles," p. 257. "To actualize" is used for the verb *vollziehen*. Note also that here and in Heidegger's 1922 essay *Leben* ("life"), *Bewegung* ("motion"), and *Augenblick* ("the moment") are likewise the terms he uses to translate respectively Aristotle's terms βίος, κίνησις, and καιρός. Regarding *Zeitigung* and *Vollzug*, see also endnote 3.

27. The German phrase is *jeweils unser eigenes Dasein*.

28. The German phrase is *jeweilen das eigene Dasein*.

29. "Position for looking," "position of looking," and "position which looks at" have been used for *Blickstellung* and *Blickstand*, since as Heidegger makes clear in §17B he means by these terms not simply a reflective and deliberately adopted epistemological "standpoint," but more literally and in a deeper sense a "position" (*Stellung*) and "state" (*Stand*) of interpretive "looking" (*Blicken*) or "seeing" (*Sehen*) which we are in "at the particular time," which is part of our historical facticity, and which, so Heidegger maintains in the present section and in §§9, 15, and 17, the method of straightforward "seeing" in previous phenomenology naively and fatefully overlooked. What is meant by these terms is closer to Aristotle's description of each of the modes of knowing and truth (the so-called "intellectual virtues") as a ἕξις ("state of having," "habit"), a term which Heidegger cites in §24, translates as *Gewohnheit* ("habit," "custom," see pp. 66, 75, 80), and uses in conjunction with ἀλήθεια ("truth" in the sense of a state of the "uncoveredness" of beings) to describe everyday "familiarity" with the world and "knowing one's way around" in it. See "Phänomenologische Interpretationen zu Aristoteles," p. 260: "Φρόνησις [practical wisdom] is a ἕξις [state], a how of having available the true safekeeping of being. And as a ἕξις, it is a γινόμενον τῆς ψυχῆς [having-become of the soul] which temporalizes itself and unfolds itself in life itself as its own possibility, brings life into a definite state [*Stand*]. . . ." Other key terms which are formed from *blicken* ("to look") and *sehen* ("to see," "look") and are used in conjunction with those above have been translated as follows: *Blick (auf)* ("looking [in the direction of, toward, at]," "view"), *Hinblick auf* ("point of view which looks in the direction of and at"), *Blickbahn (auf)* ("path of looking [toward]"), *Blickfeld* ("horizon of looking"), *Blickrichtung auf* ("direction of looking toward"), *Blicktendenz auf* ("tendency of looking toward"), *Im-Blick-halten* ("holding-in-view"), *Augenblick* ("how matters look in the moment"), *hinsehen (auf)* ("to look [in the direction of, toward, at]"), *Hinsehen (auf)* ("looking [in the direction of, toward, at]," "seeing"), *(im) Absehen (Absicht) (auf)* ("with a view to," "being-with-a-view-to," "purpose"),

Hinsicht ("point of view"), *Vorsicht (auf)* ("foresight [with respect to]"), *Gesichtsfeld* ("horizon"). For the sense in which Heidegger uses this family of ocular terms in connection with interpretation in hermeneutics, see especially §§9–10 and 15–18 in the body of the text, endnote 3, and Translator's Epilogue.

30. In connection with the use of "our own" for *eigen* in this passage, the respective translations of *Aneignung* and *angeeignet* as "appropriation" and "appropriated" should be taken in the literal sense of "making (something) our own" and "made our own."

31. The German phrase is *in seinem* jeweiligen *"Da."*

32. *Eine Bestimmung der Jeweiligkeit ist das* Heute, *das Je-Verweilen in Gegenwart, der je eigenen.*

33. See endnote 62 regarding the expression "from out of (the world)" (*von, aus*) which is reintroduced in §§18ff., as well as regarding the related term "absorption (in the world)" (*Aufgehen*) which occurs later in the present section and is reintroduced in §26 and section XII of the Appendix.

34. *Öffentlichkeit* has usually been rendered as "publicness" or "the public realm," but in the present passage and in a few other occurrences "the open space of publicness" is used in order to alert the reader to the German term's literal meaning of "openness," to Heidegger's theme in the present section and §§11–12, 18, and 26 that the today's "open space of publicness" is that wherein Dasein "whiles" (see endnotes 3, 9, and 22), and to the connection in the present section and elsewhere between this quasi-spatial term and those of "being-*there* (for a while in the today's open space of publicness)," "the there," "initial givens which are closest to us" (*Zunächst*), and "to circumscribe" (*umgrenzen*). Note also that in the introduction to Part One Heidegger uses the verb "to open up (the there of Dasein)" (*öffnen*) and that in §2 he defines Aristotle's term ἀλήθεια ("truth") as "being there out in the open" (*offen da seiend*). For the later use of *Öffentlichkeit* in connection with the "disclosedness" (*Erschlossenheit*), "being-open" (*Offensein*), and "factical spatiality" of Dasein, see endnotes 62 and 75.

35. The neologistic German phrase is *Zunächst als Zumeist*. It means that what is "initially given as closest to us" (*zunächst*) is also given "for the most part" (*zumeist*). The latter means both "given day after day" in the sense of Heidegger's term *Alltäglichkeit* ("everydayness") and "given for most of us" in the sense of his term *das Man* ("the every-one"), which is also introduced in the present sentence. In this course, as in *Being and Time*, Heidegger accordingly uses the compound phrase *zunächst und zumeist*, which has been translated as "initially and for the most part." When occurring on its own, *zunächst* is rendered with "initially" and "closest to us." The adjective *nächste* which occurs in §§18ff. is similarly translated with "closest to us" and "immediate." The noun *Zunächst* has been rendered consistently as "initial givens which are closest to us." "Initial givens now and soon to come which are closest to us" is used for *Zunächst und Demnächst* in §18. When occurring on its own, *zumeist* is rendered as "for the most part" or as "for most of us." The noun *Zumeist* is subsequently rendered as "for-the-most-part." For the spatial meaning of the above terms which are formed from the superlative *nächst* ("closest," "nearest") and are used in the last two chapters of the text in connection with Dasein's "factical spatiality," see endnote 75.

36. In order to express the average, public, and anonymous manner of Dasein's being-interpreted in the "today," Heidegger coins the noun *das Man* from the

indefinite pronoun *man*, which could be rendered as "one," "everyone," "they," "people," or even "it." *Man sagt* . . . means "one says that . . . ," "everyone says that . . . ," "they say that . . . ," "people say that . . . ," or "it is said that. . . ." Likewise, *das tut man nicht* means "one does not do that," "no one does that," "they do not do that," "people do not do that," or "it is not done." *Das Man* has been translated consistently in hyphenated form as "the every-one" in order to maintain its connection with Heidegger's use in §§21–26 of the term *man selbst* ("one-self") to characterize the worldly formation of the self on the basis of the averageness, publicness, and anonymity of "the every-one" (see endnote 62). Since he usually uses *man* as a technical term throughout his course, "everyone" and "one" have been reserved for it.

37. *"The* 'no-one'" translates "*das 'Niemand.'*" When asked "who told you so?" one can answer in German *"Herr Niemand"* ("Mr. No-One") or *"ein großer Niemand"* ("a great No-One"), whereas in English one might say "a little bird," "I heard it on the grapevine," or perhaps "no one in particular." The German phrase *der böse Niemand* (literally "the evil No-One") has the religious meaning of "the evil One," "Old Nick," or "the Tempter."

38. The German phrase is *das jeweilige Heute.*

39. *Die Hinsicht, das* Woraufhin *des An-sehens, in die jede Kultur gestellt wird.* . . . See endnote 3 regarding *das Woraufhin* ("the with-respect-to-which and on-the-basis-of-which").

40. *(Ordnung—Gestalterfassung. 1. Ordnung, 2. Ordnung, und schärfer: Idee von Kultur überhaupt; Konsequenz; Gegenpol.)*

41. In connection with n. 4 in the present section, it should be noted that Heidegger also used "Introduction" to cite his 1922 essay on Aristotle (see endnote 1) which had the same title as his lecture course in the winter semester of 1921–22, drew heavily on it, and served as the "introduction" to a large planned, though never published book on Aristotle and the history of ontology and logic which was to have worked up his course manuscripts on Aristotle into publishable form. The first section of the Appendix may be alluding to this planned book when, as the editor notes in her Table of Contents, it seems to refer to a "plan (for a book?)." For Heidegger's use of "Introduction" as an abbreviated citation of his 1922 essay, see Kisiel, *The Genesis of Heidegger's Being and Time*, p. 463, n. 12.

42. The German phrase is *das jeweilige Dasein.*

43. *Das jeweilige Dasein ist da in seiner Jeweiligkeit. Diese wird mitbestimmt durch das jeweilige Heute des Daseins. Das Heute ist das heutige Heute.*

44. The German phrase is *das Sich-da-haben des Da-seins.*

45. The present chapter uses a large number of words which are formed from *halten* ("to hold"). For their translation, interconnection, and relation to *Verweilen* ("whiling," "tarrying for a while"), see endnote 9.

46. Regarding the etymological connection between *Weg* ("path") and *Bewegtheit* ("movement"), see endnote 3.

47. *Im Zusammenhang damit steht die Aufgabe der Klärung des* Grundphänomens des *"Da" und die kategorial-ontologische Charakteristik des Da-seins.*

48. Here and elsewhere "to bring into true safekeeping" is used for *verwahren* since Heidegger intends it not only in its common meaning of "safekeeping," but also in its literal meaning of "being-true" or, in archaic terms, "betrothing." In his essay from the previous year, "Phänomenologische Interpretationen zu Aris-

toteles," Heidegger used it extensively to translate Aristotle's term ἀληθεύειν (being-true). *Bewahren* in the first section of the Appendix has likewise been rendered as "true safeguarding."

49. *Die* Vorhabe, *die ausgelegt werden soll, muß in den Gegenstandszusammenhang hineingesehen werden.*

50. The German phrase is *jeweilig eigenes Dasein.*

51. *Ausbildung des Standpunkts ist das erste im Sein. Das rechte, das die Vorurteile kennen muß, und zwar nicht nur gehaltlich, sondern im Sein. Öffentliche Toleranz; gegen sie das zuvor echte in die Welt kommen, sie frei geben.*

52. The German phrase is *das jeweilige Dasein.*

53. *Welt ist, was begegnet.* Whereas in English we would say "the world is something we encounter," in Heidegger's German sentence, which employs the verb *begegnen* ("to encounter") according to normal usage, the subject and object of the verb are reversed and the sentence literally says "the world is what en-counters (us)" in the sense of "happens (to us)." Moreover, here and often elsewhere Heidegger does not state the object of the verb (e.g., "us," "one"), so that the above sentence reads, even more literally, simply as "the world is what en-counters" or "happens." Thus, in Heidegger's use of it here, the German verb *begegnen* is far less "subjective" than the English verb "to encounter," since the world is performing an action on the human subject and the latter is in fact sometimes not even mentioned directly. It is also far more dynamic, since it has the indicative meaning of "to happen (to me for a while at the particular time)" and is thus connected to Heidegger's term "be-ing" (see endnote 5) and to what he says in §§3 and 25 about the "temporality of the world's being-encountered" and of Dasein's "being-encountered" in their "unpredictability," "incalculability," and "strange" character. In fact, all the above points should be kept in mind when in §§3ff. Heidegger deals with "Dasein's self-encounter [*Selbstbegegnung*]" and the "fundamental experience" in which *das Dasein ihm selbst begegnet* (p. 14), a phrase which, like the one discussed above, has the literal dynamic and non-subjective meaning of "Dasein happens to itself," even though it has been rendered more fully as "Dasein is encountering itself."

Heidegger understands *begegnen* ("to happen," "encounter") in the "middle voice," such that it means both (1) the passivity of having our factical historical "being-there" and that of the world "happen to" us and (2) our activity of "encountering" our "being-there" and that of the world (regarding the latter meaning, see endnote 16 on Heidegger's theme that hermeneutics involves a "wakefulness" for facticity and an "initial engagement and bringing into play" [*Einsatz*] of it). In his first lecture course of 1919, he had used the terms "it worlds" (*es weltet*) and "it happens" (*es ereignet sich*) to express this dynamic middle-voice sense of our immediate encounter with the world. See *Gesamtausgabe*, Vols. 56-57: *Zur Bestimmung der Philosophie* (Frankfurt: Klostermann, 1987), pp. 70-76. In place of these earlier terms from 1919, including the noun *Ereignis* ("happening," "event") which resurfaced as a central concept in his later writings, Heidegger began using *begegnen* and *Begegnis* ("happening," "event") as technical terms in the early twenties. Where he had spoken earlier of *Ereignischarakter* ("the character of a happening"), the present course speaks in §§18 and 26 of *Begegnischarakter* ("the character of being-encountered").

It is in order to express something of the dynamic middle-voice meaning of *begegnen* that the German sentence at the start of this endnote is translated as "The world is something being encountered" and that elsewhere *begegnen* is likewise usually translated as "is (are) (something) being encountered." "(Which is [are]) being encountered" is generally used for the adjective *begegnend,* "what is (something) being encountered" for *Begegnendes,* and "being-encountered" for *Begegnen, Begegnis,* and *Begegnung.* "Happens to be encountered" has sometimes been employed for *begegnen* since it expresses not only the dynamic middle-voice meaning of the German term but also the "unpredictability" and "incalculability" of Dasein's and the world's "being-encountered" (§§3 and 25).

54. See endnote 75 regarding the quasi-spatial terms used in the present section in connection with "spatiality": *Umwelt* ("environing world," "world round-about"), *das Umhaftes* ("environs, the round-about"), *Worin* ("the wherein"), *Woraus* ("the wherefrom, out-of-which, and on-the-basis-of-which"), and *Zunächst und Demnächst* ("initial givens now and soon to come which are closest to us").

55. The German phrase is *des "in" einer Welt Sein.* Here and in §26 (see endnote 77), Heidegger gives different formulations of the phrase *Sein in einer Welt* ("being in a world") with which the present section began, doing so in order to accentuate either the component of "in" (e.g., *in-einer-Welt-Sein* ["being-'in'-a-world"]) or that of "being" (e.g., *Sein-in-einer-Welt* ["'being'-in-a-world"]). Since it is not possible to reproduce the full force of these accentuations in the renditions I have used, the German text is provided between brackets in the body or in an endnote. See also the occurrence of the phrase *in der Welt sein* ("being 'in' the world") at the beginning of §6.

56. From this point onward, *Dasein* is translated mainly as "being-there," since Heidegger draws heavily on this literal meaning of the German term and, as he explains in the following sentence, uses this literal meaning to talk about the "being-there (for a while at the particular time)" of both the world and human life. See also endnote 7 regarding *Dasein.*

57. In the German edition, the last two terse and difficult sentences read as follows: *Die Jeweiligkeit besagt eine umgrenzte Lage, in der die Alltäglichkeit sich befindet, umgrenzt durch ein jeweiliges Zunächst, das da ist in einem Verweilen bei ihm. Dieses Verweilen bei- hat seine Weile, das Aufenthaltsmäßige der Zeitlichkeit der Alltäglichkeit, ein Verweilen bei- in einem Sichhinziehen der Zeitlichkeit.*

58. Regarding "going about dealings" (*Umgang*), see endnote 75.

59. In his 1922 essay "Phänomenologische Interpretationen zu Aristoteles," pp. 255ff., Heidegger had translated the term νοεῖν in Parmenides and Aristotle as both *Vernehmen* ("perceiving") and *Vermeinen* ("meaning [something]"). In the present text, he combines these two translations in the phrase *vernehmendes Vermeinen,* for which "perceptual mean-ing" has been used. The hyphenated term "mean-ing" has been employed to indicate that Heidegger has in mind the *act* of "mean-ing" or intending as opposed "the meaning" which is meant or intended. "Mean-ing" has also been used for the earlier related occurrences of *Meinen* in §1 and of *meinend* in §10.

60. In the present section and in §24, Heidegger uses the hyphenated verb *be-deuten* and other hyphenated terms formed from it (*Be-deuten, Be-deutsames*), so that their meaning includes both "to signify" (*bedeuten*) and more literally "to point" (*deuten*). All such occurrences have been translated with the use of both

"to signify" and "to point." See section XII of the Appendix for Heidegger's use of the stem *deuten* by itself along with *bedeuten*.

61. The German phrase is *des jeweiligen Bedeutsamen*.

62. "Availability in advance" and "advance appearance" have been used respectively for *Vorhandenheit* and *Vorschein*. As is made clear by the hyphenation of *Vorschein* in the present sentence and by the subsequent use of both terms, Heidegger exploits the literal meaning of their prefix *vor* ("fore," "in advance") in order to make the point that the disclosedness and being-interpreted of "ready-to-hand" things in the "environing world" (i.e., "availability") and that of others in the "with-world" (i.e., "appearance") always go in advance of the concrete dealings of concern (*Besorgen*) and guide them. Thus in the present chapter and in §§6 and 18, he states that this advance interpretive disclosedness of the world is that "wherefrom, out of which, and on the basis of which" (*woraus*) concern lives "for a while at the particular time." In connection with his theme of the dynamic intentional-directional sense of the interpretation of the be-ing of facticity (see endnote 3) as well as that of "factical spatiality" in §§18 and 26 (see endnote 75), he more fully defines the world's advance disclosedness as the "whereto" or "toward-which" (*Worauf*) of Dasein's "being-out-for and going-toward," the "there" of Dasein's "being-there (for a while at the particular time)," the "open space of its publicness," the "wherein" (*Worin*) of its "be-ing in a world" and its "sojourning" and "whiling," the "about-which" (*worum*) of its "caring about" (*Sorgen um*), the "around" or "round-about" (*Um*) of its "going around," and as such the advance "wherefrom, out-of-which, and on-the-basis-of-which" (*Woraus*) of its concern living "from out of" it. Accordingly, in the present section and in §23 he uses the expressions *Sorgensvorhabe* ("forehaving of caring"), *begegnenlassendes . . . Offensein . . . für Erschlossenheit* ("a being-open . . . for disclosedness . . . which lets something be encountered"), *Vor-sorge* ("fore-care"), and *Vor-begegnen* ("being-encountered-in-advance") to signal a theme explained more fully in the concluding section, i.e., that it is care as a "forehaving," "fore-care," or "being-open" which in advance discloses the there of the world's disclosedness by "be-ing in" it, "putting it in place" (*Herstellen*), "temporalizing" it, "going around" in it, "actualizing" it in the concrete dealings of concern, and "letting it be encountered" in these dealings. As Heidegger explains, care in fact "becomes absorbed" (*geht auf*) in the world's advance disclosedness, "falls away" (*fällt ab*) from itself into it, and winds up "being-encountered-in-advance" in terms of it as a worldly "one-self" (*man selbst*), i.e., as a "self" which is statically defined both in terms of the "availability in advance" of things ready-to-hand in the environing world and in terms of the "advance appearance" of the "everyone" (*Man*) in the with-world, and which accordingly becomes an object of "anxious concern and its (worldly) apprehensions" (*Besorgnis*).

63. In taking up the previous description of Heidegger's home in §20 as an illustration of the be-ing of facticity in the "awhileness of its temporal particularity" and now making it the subject matter of ontological interpretation, the final chapter reintroduces many of the colloquial terms and phrases used there. Accordingly, my translation of this chapter reproduces as exactly as possible the translations of the relevant German terms and phrases I used in §20. However, even in the German edition, the terminological connections are not always easy to see for two reasons:

First, the present chapter often does not use quotation marks when it reintroduces text from §20. For example, "used to . . . [*gebraucht zu-*], no longer really suitable for [*geeignet für*] . . ." in the present sentence (see also the opening of §23) reintroduces: "Its standing-there in the room means: Playing this role in such and such characteristic use [*Gebrauch*]. This and that about it is 'impractical,' unsuitable [*ungeeignet*]." Another good example is the following string of words which occurs a few sentences later in the present paragraph: "Temporality: there from that time, for, during, for the sake of." Here, "there from that time" (*von damals da*) reintroduces "what stands there [*da*] are . . . the skis from that time [*von damals*], from that daredevil trip with so and so" and "there at the table . . . such and such discussion that time [*damals*], there that decision . . . that time, there that *work* . . . that time, there that *holiday* . . . that time." "(There) for [*für*]" probably refers back to "Where it stood before was not at all good (for [*für*] . . .)" and "(there) during [*bei*]" probably to "Everyone sees [that it is a table *in order to* write, have a meal, sew, play] right away, e.g., during [*bei*] a visit." In another string of words near the end of the present paragraph, where Heidegger is referring back to "the books" in his home, "not yet, to be . . . for the first time" (*noch nicht, erst zu*) reintroduces "I still need to read this one for the first time [*erst noch*]." It is also reintroduced by "as not yet, as to be . . . for the first time" (*als noch nicht, als erst zu-*), which occurs in a string of temporal predicates at the start of §26. Even when Heidegger uses quotation marks, it is still not immediately clear that he is reintroducing material. For example, "'no longer' serves as means to, 'stands, lies around,' 'in the way,' junk—the 'there'" near the end of the present paragraph and "'stands in the way,' 'comes at an inconvenient time,' 'is uncomfortable,' 'disturbing,' 'awkward'" in the analysis of the "strange" in §25 are elaborations on the table's standing now "in a better spot in the room than before—there's better lighting, for example," its being nonetheless "damaged" here and there, and its possibly "being encountered again after many years when, having been taken apart and now unusable, it is found lying on the floor somewhere," as well as elaborations on the "plaything, worn out and almost unrecognizable," the "old pair of skis" (one of which is "broken in half"), the book which "needs to be taken to [the bookbinder] soon," the one "I have been wrestling [with] for a long time," and the one which "was an *unnecessary* buy, a flop."

Second, many of the colloquial terms in §20 are now reintroduced by being fashioned into neologistic technical terms without this always being clearly indicated. For example, the verb "to be there" (*dasein*) and the nouns "the there" (*Da*) and "beings-which-are-there" (*Daseiendes*) which are used frequently in this chapter refer back to "what is there [*ist da*] in *the* room there [*da*] at home is *the* table" and other colloquial uses of *da* and *dasein* in §20. In §§21–23, "being-there-in-order-to-do-this" (*Da-zu-sein*), "the in-order-to" (*Dazu*), "being-there-for-this" (*Da-für-dasein*), "the for-what" (*Dafür*), and variations of these terms reintroduce "*the* table . . . at which one sits *in order to* [zum] write, have a meal, sew, play" and "Where it stood before was not at all good (for [*für*] . . .)." The terms "one" [*man*] and "one-self" [*man selbst*], which are used throughout the present chapter and are related to the term "the every-one" (*Man*) introduced in §6 and mentioned again at the start of §18, refer back to: ". . . *the* table . . . at which one [*man*] sits *in order to* write, have a meal, sew, play. Everyone [*Man*] sees this right away. . . . My library is not as good as A's but far better than B's, this matter is not something one [*man*] would be able to derive pleasure from, what will the others say about this way of doing it [*was werden die anderen zu dieser Aufmachung sagen*]." Parts of this passage are also reintroduced in the present section in the phrase "the path of heeding what the others say about it [*was die anderen dazu sagen*]" and in the sentence "Whatever one-self is . . . defines itself from out of and on the basis of what one in advance comes to appearance as with the others and in contrast to *them.*"

64. The German phrase is *ins Da drängend*. In §§21 and 23, Heidegger uses the verbs *drängen, aufdrängen,* and *hereindrängen* to talk about how things and persons "press forth" into their "there" and respectively into their "availability" and "appearance." All three verbs have been translated as "to press (forth)." The same translation was used for the earlier occurrence of *drängen* in §7 in the context of Heidegger's discussion of the concept of "expression" in historical consciousness. "Oppressiveness" and "something oppressive" have been used for the related terms *Aufdringlichkeit* and *Aufdringliches* in §25.

65. The German edition reproduces Heidegger's hand-drawn line as presented here.

66. "Anxious concern and its apprehensions" translates *Besorgnis*. See endnote 17.

67. Regarding "one-self" (*man selbst*) and its connection to "the every-one" (*das Man*), see endnotes 36 and 62.

68. *Wichtig für das Worauf des Ausseins: Vor-sorge und ihr "um."* Regarding the term *Vor-sorge* ("fore-care") in this sentence, as well as the related term *Vor-begegnen* ("being-encountered-in-advance") in the following sentence, see endnote 62. Regarding *ihr "um"* ("its 'about,' what it goes 'around' in") in the above sentence, see endnote 75 on *um*.

69. The German phrase is *einer jeweiligen* Vertrautheit.

70. *Jeder kennt sich jeweilig aus, is bekannt mit anderen, so wie die anderen mit ihm.*

71. Regarding the way that this passage reintroduces text from §20, see endnote 63.

72. Regarding the way that this sentence reintroduces text from §20, see endnote 63.

73. The German phrase is *in der jeweiligen* Sorge.

74. The entire sentence reads: *Im vorhinein sind das Wofür und Wozu und seine mitweltlichen Anderen das, worum es in der Sorge geht.* See the following endnote on "spatiality" regarding Heidegger's use of *wo* ("where") in this sentence and in the preceding one, as well as for an explanation of why the polysemantic phrase *das, worum es in der Sorge geht* in the above sentence is translated as "that about which care is concerned, that wherein it goes around."

75. *Dieses im Verweisungszusammenhang hin-und-her-Gehen charakterisiert* Sorgen als Umgehen. As Heidegger's use of the preposition *um* ("about," "around") especially in this sentence, in the previous paragraph, and in §23 (see endnote 68) makes clear, he sometimes intends it to have both (1) the intentional-directional meaning of "about" in the sense of "care about" (*Sorge um*), being "concerned about" (*besorgt um*), or "that about which care is concerned" (*das, worum es in der Sorge geht*) and (2) the spatial meaning of "around" in the sense of "going around" (*Umgehen*) or the "world around us" (*Umwelt*) as the "wherein" of our "being in a world," of our "sojourning" and "whiling" "at the particular time."

The latter meaning is connected to the theme of "factical spatiality" which was introduced in §18 and is reintroduced in the following paragraph in the present section. The main reason for Heidegger's use of the above double meaning of *um* is that he wants to make the point that what is spatially "around" us, i.e., the "there" of the "world around us," is always at the same time what we intentionally care "about" or are concerned "about," and vice-versa. Putting this in other terms, the world as the spatial "wherein" (*Worin*) of our "being in a world" is at the same time the intentional "whereto" or "toward-which" (*Worauf*) of our care, and vice versa. Regarding these intentional-directional and spatial dimensions of "being in a world," see endnotes 3 and 62. Thus in the present section and in previous ones, where *um* is used frequently as a preposition, as a component of a noun or verb, and as itself a noun, the following translations, many of which use both "around" and "about," have been employed:

Uses of "um" with Sorge. In the previous paragraph, the phrase *das, worum es in der Sorge geht* has two meanings: (1) the intentional-directional meaning of "that which it is all about in care," "that which is gone about in care," or "that about which care is concerned" and (2) the spatial meaning of "that wherein things move in care" or, more simply, "that wherein care goes around." To complicate matters even more, Heidegger also has in mind the spatial dimension in the literal meaning of the conjunctive *worum* ("whereabout") and of the following conjunctives used in the same paragraph and in the following one: *worin*, which has been translated literally as "wherein"; *Wofür*, which has the literal archaic meaning of "the wherefore," but has consistently been translated as "the for-what"; *Wozu*, which means literally "the whereto," but has consistently been translated as "the in-order-to"; and *Womit*, which means literally "the wherewith," but has been translated as "the with-which." For the above two reasons, the phrase *das, worum es in der Sorge geht* has been rendered as "that about which care is concerned, that wherein it goes around." Similarly, *Vor-sorge und ihr "um"* in §23 has been translated as "fore-care and its 'about,' what it goes 'around' in" (see endnote 68). Note that, even though Heidegger does not use the preposition *um* ("about") with them, *besorgen* is rendered as "to be concerned about and attend to," *Besorgtes* as "what we are concerned about and attend to," *Besorgtsein* as "being-of-concern" and "being-attended-to," and *Besorgen* either as "concern," "being-concerned-about," or "being concerned about and attending to." These renditions have been used for two reasons. First, they felicitously help establish the first of the two meanings of *um* as "(care or concern) about." Second, and more importantly, they express something of the strong transitive meaning of the German terms they translate. *Etwas besorgen* means to "procure" or "attend" something and is used by Heidegger in connection with the term *Aufgehen in* ("absorption in" in the literal sense of "going [transitively] straight into" something) which occurs in §§6 and 26. *Etwas besorgen* does not have the intransitive and reflexive sense of the English expression "to concern oneself with something." A literal translation using "to concern" would in fact have to be something like "I concern something." Nor is the verbal and transitive meaning of the gerund *Besorgen* ("procuring," "attending") captured by the static and subject-oriented term "(our) concern," which is the conventional English translation I have sometimes used. Regarding "care" and "concern," see also endnotes 17 and 62.

Uses of "um" as prefix. Depending on the context, either "dealing(s)," "going about dealings," or "going around" is employed for *Umgang,* a term which occurs throughout Heidegger's course. By itself, however, "going about dealings" is intended to express not only the German term's conventional meaning of "dealings," but also something of its literal meaning of "going around" or "circulating." The two occurrences of the gerund *Umgehen* in §21 have been translated as "going-around (in dealings)." Its occurrence in the sentence quoted at the start of this endnote has been rendered as "going about dealings in the sense of a going around." *Umwelt* in the present section and in §18 is rendered as "environing world, world round-about" or simply as "environing world." The use of "world round-about" is intended to convey the double meaning of *um* ("around," "about") in *Umwelt* and should be read as expressing the point that the world which is "around" us is also a world "about" which we care or are concerned in our dealings with it, and vice versa. In §21, "sphere (of others)" is used for *Umkreis* and "stands, lies around" for *steht, liegt herum.* "To circumscribe (the there, possibility, sight, situation, etc.)" is used for occurrences of *umgrenzen* in the introduction to Part One and in §§3, 6, 18, and 21.

"Um" as noun. In addition to the above-mentioned use of "its 'about,' what it goes 'around' in" for the noun *ihr "um"* in §23 (see endnote 68), "the roundabout" and "environs" are used for the *das Um* in §26 and in section XII of the Appendix and for *das Umhafte* in §§18, 21, and 26.

Connected Spatial Terms: "wo," "nächst," and "Öffentlichkeit." Especially in §18 and in the present section, Heidegger uses a number of conjunctives containing *wo* ("where") as well as nouns coined from these conjunctives in order to describe different dimensions of the world as the "where" or "there" of Dasein's "whiling" "at the particular time." So as to maintain their connection with the above spatial terms formed from *um* ("around"), other spatial terms, and the general theme of "spatiality" in the present section, I have used "where" in the following ways when this was possible and appropriate: *woraus* ("wherefrom, out of which, and on the basis of which"), *Woraus* ("the wherefrom, out-of-which, and on-the-basis-of-which"), *worin* ("wherein"), *Worin* ("the wherein"), *worauf* ("whereto"), *Worauf* ("the whereto," "toward-which"), *worum* ("wherein," "about which"). As for *Wofür, Wozu,* and *Womit,* which occur in the present and preceding paragraphs in Heidegger's text, it was not possible to use archaic English conjunctives to provide the following respective literal translations of them: "the wherefore," "the whereto," and "the wherewith." Rather, "the for-what," "the in-order-to," and "the with-which" were used in the present and previous sections. Nor was *worum* in the above-discussed phrase *das, worum es in der Sorge geht* able to be translated literally and archaically as "whereabout" ("that whereabout care is concerned"). Rather, as explained, "about which" and "wherein" ("that about which care is concerned, that wherein it goes around") had to be used. The reader should nonetheless keep in mind the above literal archaic translations.

Note also the following terms which are formed from the superlative *nächst* ("nearest," "closest") and have been used in the last two chapters in connection with Dasein's spatiality: *nächste* ("closest to us," "immediate"), *zunächst* ("closest to us," "initially"), and *Zunächst und Demnächst* ("initial givens now and soon to come which are closest to us"). See also endnote 35 regarding these terms. Finally, note that the present section reintroduces the term *Öffentlichkeit* in connection with Dasein's spatiality and plays on its literal meaning of "openness." It is thus translated both as "publicness" and as "the open space of publicness." See also endnote 34 regarding "the open space of publicness."

76. The German phrase is *eine jeweilige Vertrautheit mit ihren Verweisungen*.

77. *Es gibt die Möglichkeit, die ontologische Bedeutung des In- und Innerhalb-einer-Welt zu interpretieren. In-der-Welt-sein besagt nicht: Vorkommen unter anderen Dingen, sondern heißt: das Um der begegnenden Welt besorgend bei ihm Verweilen. Das eigentliche Weise des Seins selbst in einer Welt ist das* Sorgen. . . . See endnote 55 on Heidegger's different formulations of the phrase *Sein in einer Welt* ("being in a world").

78. *Leben besorgt sich selbst und, da die Sorge jeweilig ihre Sprache hat, spricht es sich dabei weltlich an.*

79. See n. 4 in §9 and endnote 41 for the editor's surmise that Heidegger may be referring to a "plan" for a book here.

80. See Translator's Epilogue regarding the idiosyncratic system of indentation and line breaks in Heidegger's very rough notes which are presented in the Appendix.

81. Upon my inquiry about the meaning of "E" in the last paragraph of this insert, Heidegger's son and literary executor, Hermann Heidegger, stated in his letter that neither he nor the German editor were able to solve this riddle. So "E" was simply reproduced in the German edition of Heidegger's text. So far as I was able to determine by carefully studying both a photocopy of the manuscript page and its edited form, the "A" which occurs a few lines above refers to the first item in a list and the "E" in the last paragraph probably to the fifth item, even though "B," "C," and "D" do not occur to mark the intervening items. In the manuscript, a space of at least six lines was left between the last two paragraphs and was perhaps intended for the subsequent insertion of one or more of the intervening items. "Going back to A" in the last paragraph which begins with "E" is probably a reference back to the first item in the list.

82. In Heidegger's manuscript, this line is followed by the line "The today — philosophy — curiosity — s. above." This suggests even more strongly that this page of notes is referring back to §8 on "philosophy" and §7 on "historical conscious- ness" and taking Husserl and Dilthey as respective representatives of these two approaches.

83. "Dilthey, laying a foundation" translates *Dilthey, Grundlegung*, though the latter is perhaps Heidegger's abbreviated citation of Dilthey's *Einleitung in die Geisteswissenschaften: Versuch einer Grundlegung für das Studium der Gesellschaft und der Geschichte* [*Introduction to the Human Sciences: An Attempt to Lay a Foundation for the Study of Society and History*], which was cited earlier in n. 1 in §14.

84. The German phrase is *im jeweiligen Lebenszusammenhang*.

85. The German phrase is *vom jeweiligen genuinen "Aufenthalt."*

86. The German title uses parenthesis: *Ontologie (Hermeneutik der Faktizität)*. See also endnote 1 for an explanation of Heidegger's different course titles.

Glossary

The following glossary lists only the most important or problematic German expressions and their English translations. The German-English section does not list every English rendering of a given German expression. Likewise, the English-German section does not list every German expression which an English word translates.

German-English

Abbau: dismantling
abbauen: to dismantle
Abfall: falling away
abheben (erheben, herausheben): to bring into relief
(im) Absehen (Absicht) (auf): with a view to, being-with-a-view-to, purpose
absichtlich: intentionally with a view to
alltäglich: everyday
Alltäglichkeit: everydayness
als was (n.): the as what
aneignen: to appropriate
aneignend: appropriate (adj.)
Aneignung: appropriation, appropriating
angemessen: fitting, appropriate
Angst: anxiety
ankommen: to be at issue (be about) and come to
Ansatz: (initial) approach, starting point
ansprechen: to address
Anweisung: directive
(formale) Anzeige: (formal) indication
anzeigen: to indicate
anzeigend: indicative
auf: with respect to, on the basis of, and with a view to; in the direction of, toward, to, at
aufdecken: to uncover
Aufdringlichkeit: oppressiveness
Aufenthalt: sojourn, halting, holding out, abode
aufenthaltslos: abode-less; never halting, making a sojourn, and holding out there
auffassen: to comprehend
Auffassung: comprehension

Aufgehen: absorption
(sich) aufhalten: to hold itself and sojourn
Aufhalten (bei): sojourning (at home in), holding itself (in), holding out (in)
Augenblick: how matters look in the moment
aus: (from) out of, on the basis of; from out of and on the basis of
ausbilden: to develop, work out
Ausbildung: developing, working out
Ausdruck: expression
ausdrücklich: explicit
Ausdrucksein: being-an-expression, expressive being
Ausgang: point of departure
Ausgelegtheit: (manner, state of) having-been-interpreted, being-interpreted
aushalten: to hold out
(sich) auskennen: to know one's way around
auslegen (auf): to interpret, explicate interpretively (with respect to, on the basis of, and with a view to)
Auslegung: interpretation
Auslegungsrichtung: direction of interpretation
ausrechnen im vorhinein: to calculate and work out in advance
aussein auf: to be out for and going toward
Aussein auf: being-out-for and going-toward
ausweisen: to demonstrate

bedeuten: to signify, mean
be-deuten: to signify and point
bedeutsam: significant

Bedeutsamkeit: significance

Bedrängnis: distress, something distressing

befragen (*auf*): to interrogate (with respect to, on the basis of, and with a view to)

begegnen: is (are) (something) being encountered, to happen to be encountered, to encounter

Begegnen: being-encountered

begegnend: which is (are) being encountered

Begegnendes: what is (something) being encountered

begegnen lassen: to let be encountered

Begegnis: being-encountered, encountering

Begegnung: being-encountered

Behaltbarkeit: ability of preservation to hold onto the past

behalten: to hold onto, preserve

bei: (at home) in, among

bekümmert: worried

Bekümmerung: worry (n.)

Beschäftigtsein: being-occupied

besorgen: to be concerned about and attend to

Besorgen: concern, being-concerned-about, being concerned about and attending to

Besorgnis: anxious concern and its apprehensions

Besorgtes: what we are concerned about and attend to

Besorgtsein: being-of-concern (and being-attended-to)

bestimmen: to define

bestimmt: definite, certain, specific

Bestimmtheit: definiteness

Bestimmung: definition

betrachten: to observe, examine

betreiben: to pursue

Betreiben: pursuits

Betrieb: industry, industriousness

Bewahren: true safeguarding

Bewegtheit: movement

Bewegung: motion

Bezogensein (*auf*): being-related (to)

Bezug (*auf*): relation (to)

Bildungsbewußtsein: educated consciousness

Blick (*auf*): looking (in the direction of, toward, at), view

Blickbahn (*auf*): path of looking (toward)

Blickfeld: horizon of looking

Blickrichtung auf: direction of looking toward

Blickstand (*Blickstellung*): position of (for) looking, position which looks at

Blicktendenz auf: tendency of looking toward

Charakter: character, characteristic

charakterisieren: characterize

da: there

Da: the there

dabeisein: to be at home there, be involved in

Da-bei-sein: being-there-at-home-in, being-there-involved-in

Da-Charakter: character of the there

Dafür: the there-for-this

Da-für-dasein (*Dafür-sein*): being-there-for-this

daraufhin (*daraufzu*): with respect to, on the basis of, and with a view to

Daseiendes: beings-which-are-there, those-who-are-there

dasein: to be there

Dasein: Dasein, being-there, the being-there of Dasein, Dasein in its being-there, being-there for Dasein

Dazu: the there-in-order-to-do-this

Da-zu-sein: being-there-in-order-to-do-this

demnächst: soon

Demnächst (*Zunächst und*): initial givens now and soon to come which are closest to us

Destruktion: destruction

destruktiv: destructive

dienlich: being a means to

Ding: thing

Dingdasein: being-there of things

drängen (*aufdrängen*, *hereindrängen*): to press forth

durchhalten: to hold out until the end

durchschnittlich: average

Durchschnittlichkeit: averageness

eigen: (our, one's) own

Eigenheit: our own

eigentlich: authentic, proper
Eigentlichkeit: authenticity
Einsatz: initial engagement and bringing into play, engaging
einsetzen: to engage itself (and bring
itself into play), to put forth initially and bring into play
entdecken: to uncover
Entdecktheit: uncoveredness
Enthalten von: holding back from
entsprechend: corresponding, appropriate
erfassen: to grasp (and record)
ergreifen: to grasp (and stir), take up
erhalten: to preserve, gain a foothold,
hold open
Erschlossenheit: disclosedness
Existenz: existence
Existenzialien: existentials
existenziell: existential
Explikation: explication
(sich) explizieren: to explicate itself, become explicit

faktisch: factical
Faktizität: facticity
festhalten: to hold fast (to)
fraglich: questionable
Fraglichkeit: questionableness
Fremdes: something strange

Gegenstandsein: being-an-object
Gegenwart: the present
gegenwärtig: present (adj.)
Gerede: talk (n.)
Gerichtetsein auf: being-directed toward
Geschichte: history
Geschichtlichkeit: historicity
Gesichtsfeld: horizon
Gestalt: form (n.)
Gewesenseiendes: beings-which-have-
been
Gewesensein: (being of) having-been
Gewohnheit: habit, custom
Grunderfahrung: fundamental experi-
ence

Halt: hold (n.)
(sich) halten: to hold (itself) (and linger)
halten an: to require to hold to
Haltung: stance held to, approach
herstellen: to produce
Herstellen: producing, putting in place
heute: today (adv.)

Heute: the today
heutig: today (adv.), today's
Hinblick auf: point of view which
looks in the direction of and at
hineinordnen: to classify and file away
hinsehen (auf): to look (in the direction of, toward, at)
Hinsehen (auf): looking (in the direction of, toward, at), seeing
Hinsicht: point of view
Horizont: horizon

Im-Blick-halten: holding-in-view
Immerdasein: always-being-there
Immersosein: always-being-in-such-a-
manner
in-der-Welt-sein: to-be-"in"-the-world
"in" einer Welt Sein: being "in" a world
In-einer-Welt-Sein: being-"in"-a-world
Innerhalb-einer-Welt-Sein: being-
"within"-a-world
"in"-Sein (In-Sein): being-"in"

je: in each case, each
jetzig: now
jetzt: now
Jetztsein: being-now
Je-Verweilen: in each case whiling, tarrying for a while
jeweilen: in each case for a while at
the particular time, for a while at
particular times, at particular
times and for a while
jeweilig (adj., adv.): in each case for a
while at the particular time, (temporally) particular, all the while,
at the particular time, at particular
times, in each particular case, respective, each
Jeweiligkeit: the awhileness (of temporal particularity)
jeweils: in each case for a while at the
particular time, at the particular
time, respectively, each

kairologisch: kairological
kundgeben: to (announce and) make
known

Lebensnähe: being true to life

man: one, everyone
Man: the every-one

man selbst (n., pron.): (the) one-self
Maske: mask, masking, masquerade
maskieren: to mask
Meinen: mean-ing
Mensch: man, human being
Menschsein: human being
Mitdaseiende: those-who-are-there-with-us
mitgehen: to become involved in
Mitlebende: those with us in life
mitteilen: to communicate
Mitwelt: with-world
mitweltlich: in the (of the) with-world
Möglichsein: being-possible
Motiv: motive
motivieren: to motivate

nachgehen: to pursue
Nachgehen: pursuing, investigating (which pursues)
nächste: closest to us, immediate
nachvollziehen: to reactivate
Neugier: curiosity
Niemand: the no-one

Offensein: being-open
öffentlich: public, in the public realm
Öffentlichkeit: (open space of) public-ness, public realm
öffnen: to open up
ontisch: ontic
ontologisch: ontological
ordnen: to classify
Ordnung: classification, classificatory order

präsent: (made) present
Präsenthaben: having-present
präsentieren: to make present (and put forward, offer, introduce)
Präsentsein: being-present
Präsenz: presence

Räumlichkeit: spatiality
Rede: discourse
repräsentieren: to make present, re-present
richten (*auf*): to direct (toward)
Richtung: direction

Sache (*selbst*): subject matter, thing (itself)
Sehen: seeing

Seiendes: beings, a being
Sein: be-ing, being
Sein in einer Welt: being in a world
Sein-in-einer-Welt: "being"-in-a-world
Seinscharakter: character (characteristic) of being
seinsmäßig: in the manner of be-ing (being)
Selbstauslegung: self-interpretation
Selbstbegegnung: self-encounter
Selbstpräsentation: self-presentation
Selbstverständigung: self-communication and self-understanding
Selbstverständlichkeit: self-evidence
Selbstwelt: self-world
Sicherheit: certainty and security
Sichselbstdahaben (*Sich-da-haben*): having-itself-there
Sichselbsthaben: having-itself
Sich-verdecken: covering-itself-up
Sichverhalten (*zu*): comportment (to-ward), comporting-itself (toward), self-comportment, holding-itself in the comportment
Sich-verschleiern: self-veiling
So: suchness
So-dasein: being-there-in-such-a-manner
So-da-sein: being-there-in-such-and-such-a-manner
Sorge: care (n.)
Sorgen: caring
Sorglosigkeit: carefreeness
So-Sehen: seeing-in-such-and-such-a-manner
Sosein: being-in-such-a-manner, being-in-such-and-such-a-manner
Sprung: leap
Stand: position (n.)
Standpunkt: standpoint
Standpunktfreiheit: freedom from standpoints
stellen: to place, put into place
Stellung: position (n.)
Stil: style
Störbarkeit: disturbability
stören: to disturb

Tendenz: tendency

Überall- und Nirgendsein: being-every-where-and-nowhere

um: around, about

Um (*um*): the round-about, environs, what it goes around in

Umgang: dealing(s), going about dealings, going around

Umgehen: going around (going-around), going about dealings

umgrenzen: to circumscribe

Umhaftes: environs, the round-about

Umwelt: environing world, world round-about

unabgehoben: inexplicit

unausdrücklich: inexplicit, not explicit

Unberechenbarkeit: unpredictability, incalculability

unbestimmt: indefinite (and vague)

unmittelbar: immediate

Unterwegs(sein): being-on-the-way

unverborgen: unconcealed

Ursprung: origin

ursprünglich: original, primordial

Ursprünglichkeit: primordiality

Verborgenes: what is concealed

verdecken: to cover up, hide

Verdeckung: covering up

Verfall: fallenness

verfolgen: to pursue

Verfolgen: pursuing, investigating (which pursues)

verfügbar: at our disposal, available

Verfügbarsein: being-at-our-disposal

vergegenwärtigen: to (make) present

Vergegenwärtigung: presenting, presentation

Verhalten: comportment, comporting

Vermeinen: mean-ing

vernehmend: perceptual

Verrichten: directing ourselves to tasks

versetzen: to transport

verstehen: to understand

Verstehen: understanding

Vertrautheit: familiarity

verwahren: to bring into true safe-keeping

Verweilen (*bei*): whiling, tarrying for a while (awhile) (at home in, among), tarrying-for-a-while, tarrying-awhile

Verweisung (*Verweis*): reference

Verweisungszusammenhang: context of references

vollziehen: to actualize

Vollzug: actualizing, actualization

Vorausberechnung: prediction and advance calculation

Vor-begegnen: being-encountered-in-advance

Vorgriff: foreconception

Vorhabe: forehaving

vorhalten: to hold up before

vorhanden: available in advance

Vorhandenheit: availability in advance

(*im*) *vorhinein*: in advance

Vorkehrung: precautionary measure

vorkommen: to come forth

(*etwas*) *Vorläufiges*: something preliminary which runs in advance

Vorschein: advance appearance

Vorsicht (*auf*): foresight (with respect to)

Vor-sorge: fore-care

Vorsprung: anticipatory leap forward and running in advance

Vorstellung: representation, presentation

Vorweghaben: anticipatory forehaving (which prepares a path in advance)

vorweglaufend: anticipatory, running in advance

Vorwegnahme: anticipatory apprehension (which prepares a path in advance)

wach: wide-awake, wakeful

Wachsein: wakefulness, being-wakeful

warnend: cautionary

Was: the what

Weg: path

Weile: while (n.)

Weise: mode, manner, way (of pointing)

Weisung: directive

Welt: world

Weltdasein: worldly being-there

Weltdasein-Sein: being a worldly being-there

weltlich: worldly

weltliches Dasein: worldly being-there

Wie: the how

Wofür: the for-what

Wohinein: the whereinto

Womit: the with-which

Worauf: the toward-which, the whereto

Woraufhin: the with-respect-to-which and on-the-basis-of-which

woraus: wherefrom, out of which, and on the basis of which
Woraus: the wherefrom, out-of-which, and on-the-basis-of-which; the out-of-which
worin: wherein
Worin: the wherein
Worüber: the about-which
worum: about which, wherein
Wozu: the in-order-to

(*eine*) *Zeit*: (a) time
zeitigen: to temporalize (and unfold)
Zeitigung: temporalizing, temporalization
Zeitlichkeit: temporality
zueignen: to appropriate
Zug: pull
Zugang: (gaining) access

Zugehen: going-toward, gaining-access-to
zuhanden: ready-to-hand
Zu-handen-da-sein: being-there-ready-to-hand
Zuhandensein: being-ready-to-hand
Zukunft: future
zumeist: for the most part, for most of us
Zumeist: for-the-most-part (and for-most-of-us)
zunächst: initially, closest to us
Zunächst: initial givens which are closest to us
Zunächst und Demnächst: initial givens now and soon to come which are closest to us
Zusammenhang: context, relation
zusehen: to look into
Zusehen: looking-into

English-German

abode: *Aufenthalt*
abode-less: *aufenthaltslos*
about: *um*
about (be a. and come to): *ankommen*
about which: *worum*
about-which (the): *Worüber*
absorption: *Aufgehen*
access (gaining): *Zugang*
actualize: *vollziehen*
actualizing (actualization): *Vollzug*
address (to): *ansprechen*
always-being-in-such-a-manner: *Immersosein*
always-being-there: *Immerdasein*
among: *bei*
announce and make known: *kundgeben*
anticipatory: *vorweglaufend*
anticipatory apprehension (which prepares a path in advance): *Vorwegnahme*
anticipatory forehaving (which prepares a path in advance): *Vorweghaben*
anticipatory leap forward and running in advance: *Vorsprung*
anxiety: *Angst*
appearance (advance): *Vorschein*
apprehensions (anxious concern and its a.): *Besorgnis*

approach (initial): *Ansatz, Haltung*
appropriate (adj.): *aneignend, entsprechend, angemessen*
appropriate (to): *aneignen*
appropriation (appropriating): *Aneignung*
around: *um*
as what (the): *als was*
at home in: *bei*
at home there (to be): *dabeisein*
attending to (being concerned about and): *Besorgen*
attend to (to be concerned about and): *besorgen*
attend to (what we are concerned about and): *Besorgtes*
authentic: *eigentlich*
authenticity: *Eigentlichkeit*
availability (in advance): *Vorhandenheit*
available (in advance): *vorhanden, verfügbar*
average: *durchschnittlich*
averageness: *Durchschnittlichkeit*
awhile (tarrying): *Verweilen*
awhileness (of temporal particularity): *Jeweiligkeit*

be-ing (being): *Sein*
being (character, characteristic of): *Seinscharakter*

be-ing (in the manner of): *seinsmäßig*
being-an-expression: *Ausdrucksein*
being-an-object: *Gegenstandsein*
being-at-our-disposal: *Verfügbarsein*
being-attended-to (being-of-concern and): *Besorgtsein*
being-concerned-about: *Besorgen*
being-directed toward: *Gerichtetsein auf*
being-encountered: *Begegnen, Begegnung, Begegnis*
being-encountered-in-advance: *Vorbegegnen*
being-everywhere-and-nowhere: *Überall- und Nirgendsein*
being-"in": *"in"-Sein, In-Sein*
being in a world: *Sein in einer Welt*
being "in" a world: *"in" einer Welt Sein*
being-"in"-a-world: *In-einer-Welt-Sein*
"being"-in-a-world: *Sein-in-einer-Welt*
being-in-such-a-manner (being-in-such-and-such-a-manner): *Sosein*
being-interpreted: *Ausgelegtheit*
being-now: *Jetztsein*
being-occupied: *Beschäfigtsein*
being-of-concern (and being-attended-to): *Besorgtsein*
being-on-the-way: *Unterwegs(sein)*
being-open: *Offensein*
being-out-for and going-toward: *Aussein auf*
being-possible: *Möglichsein*
being-present: *Präsentsein*
being-ready-to-hand: *Zuhandensein*
being-related (to): *Bezogensein (auf)*
beings (a being): *Seiendes*
beings-which-are-there: *Daseiendes*
beings-which-have-been: *Gewesenseiendes*
being-there (being a worldly): *Weltdasein-Sein*
being-there (Dasein in its b., the b. of Dasein, b. for Dasein): *Dasein*
being-there (worldly): *Weltdasein, weltliches Dasein*
being-there-at-home-in: *Da-bei-sein*
being-there-for-this: *Da-für-dasein, Dafür-sein*
being-there-in-order-to-do-this: *Da-zu-sein*
being-there-in-such-a-manner: *So-dasein*
being-there-in-such-and-such-a-manner: *So-da-sein*
being-there-involved-in: *Da-bei-sein*

being-there of things: *Dingdasein*
being-there-ready-to-hand: *Zu-handen-da-sein*
being-wakeful: *Wachsein*
being-with-a-view-to: *Absehen*
being-"within"-a-world: *Innerhalb-einer-Welt-Sein*
bring into play (put forth initially and): *einsetzen*
bringing into play (initial engagement and): *Einsatz*
bring itself into play (engage itself and): *einsetzen*

calculate and work out: *ausrechnen*
calculation (advance c. and prediction): *Vorausberechnung*
care (n.): *Sorge*
carefreeness: *Sorglosigkeit*
caring: *Sorgen*
cautionary: *warnend*
certainty and security: *Sicherheit*
character (characteristic): *Charakter*
characterize: *charakterisieren*
circumscribe: *umgrenzen*
classification (classificatory order): *Ordnung*
classify: *ordnen*
classify and file away: *hineinordnen*
closest to us: *nächste, zunächst*
closest to us (initial givens now and soon to come which are): *Zunächst und Demnächst*
closest to us (initial givens which are): *Zunächst*
come forth: *vorkommen*
come to (to be at issue [be about] and): *ankommen*
communicate: *mitteilen*
comporting (comportment): *Verhalten*
comporting-itself (comportment, self-comportment) (toward): *Sichverhalten (zu)*
comprehend: *auffassen*
comprehension: *Auffassung*
concealed (what is): *Verborgenes*
concern: *Besorgen*
concern (anxious c. and its apprehensions): *Besorgnis*
concerned about and attending to (being): *Besorgen*
concerned about and attend to (to be): *besorgen*

concerned about and attend to (what we are): *Besorgtes*
context: *Zusammenhang*
corresponding: *entsprechend*
covering-itself-up: *Sich-verdecken*
covering up: *Verdeckung*
cover up: *verdecken*
curiosity: *Neugier*
custom: *Gewohnheit*

Dasein (the being-there of D., D. in its being-there, being-there for D.): *Dasein*
dealings (going about): *Umgang, Umgehen*
define: *bestimmen*
definite: *bestimmt*
definiteness: *Bestimmtheit*
definition: *Bestimmung*
demonstrate: *ausweisen*
destruction: *Destruktion*
destructive: *destruktiv*
develop: *ausbilden*
developing: *Ausbildung*
direct (toward): *richten (auf)*
directing ourselves to tasks: *Verrichten*
direction: *Richtung*
direction of interpretation: *Auslegungsrichtung*
direction of looking toward: *Blickrichtung auf*
directive: *Anweisung, Weisung*
disclosedness: *Erschlossenheit*
discourse: *Rede*
dismantle: *abbauen*
dismantling: *Abbau*
disposal (at our): *verfügbar*
distress (something distressing): *Bedrängnis*
disturb: *stören*
disturbability: *Störbarkeit*

each: *je, jeweilig, jeweils*
educated consciousness: *Bildungsbewußtsein*
encounter (to): *begegnen*
encountered (is [are] [something] being): *begegnen*
encountered (to happen to be): *begegnen*
encountered (to let be): *begegnen lassen*
encountered (what is [something] being): *Begegnendes*

encountered (which is [are] being): *begegnend*
encountering: *Begegnis*
engage itself (and bring itself into play): *einsetzen*
engagement and bringing into play (initial): *Einsatz*
engaging: *Einsatz*
environing world: *Umwelt*
environs: *Umhaftes, Um*
everyday: *alltäglich*
everydayness: *Alltäglichkeit*
everyone (pron.): *man*
every-one (the): *Man*
existence: *Existenz*
existential: *existenziell*
existentials: *Existenzialien*
explicate interpretively: *auslegen*
explicate itself (become explicit): *sich explizieren*
explication: *Explikation*
explicit: *ausdrücklich*
expression: *Ausdruck*

factical: *faktisch*
facticity: *Faktizität*
fallenness: *Verfall*
falling away: *Abfall*
familiarity: *Vertrautheit*
file away (classify and): *hineinordnen*
fitting: *angemessen*
foothold (gain a): *erhalten*
fore-care: *Vor-sorge*
foreconception: *Vorgriff*
forehaving: *Vorhabe*
forehaving (anticipatory f. [which prepares a path in advance]): *Vorweghaben*
foresight (with respect to): *Vorsicht (auf)*
form (n.): *Gestalt*
for the most part (for most of us): *zumeist*
for-the-most-part (and for-most-of-us): *Zumeist*
for-what (the): *Wofür*
from out of (and on the basis of): *aus*
fundamental experience: *Grunderfahrung*
future: *Zukunft*

gaining-access-to: *Zugehen*
givens now and soon to come which

are closest to us (initial): *Zunächst
und Demnächst*
givens which are closest to us (initial): *Zunächst*
going around (going-around): *Umgehen*
going toward (to be out for and): *aussein auf*
going-toward: *Zugehen*
going-toward (being-out-for and):
Aussein auf
grasp (and record): *erfassen*
grasp (and stir): *ergreifen*

habit: *Gewohnheit*
halting: *Aufenthalt*
halting (never h., making a sojourn,
and holding out there): *aufenthaltslos*
having-been (being of): *Gewesensein*
having-been-interpreted (manner,
state of): *Ausgelegtheit*
having-itself: *Sichselbsthaben*
having-itself-there: *Sichselbstdahaben,
Sich-da-haben*
having-present: *Präsenthaben*
hide: *verdecken*
historicity: *Geschichtlichkeit*
history: *Geschichte*
hold (n.): *Halt*
hold (itself) (and linger): *(sich) halten*
hold fast: *festhalten*
holding back from: *Enthalten von*
holding-in-view: *Im-Blick-halten*
holding itself (in): *Aufhalten (bei)*
holding-itself in the comportment:
Sichverhalten
holding out (in): *Aufenthalt, Aufhalten
(bei)*
holding out (never halting, making a
sojourn, and h. o. there): *aufenthaltslos*
hold itself and sojourn: *sich aufhalten*
hold onto: *behalten*
hold open: *erhalten*
hold out (until the end): *aushalten,
durchhalten*
hold to (require to): *halten an*
hold up before: *vorhalten*
horizon (of looking): *Blickfeld,
Gesichtsfeld, Horizont*
how (the): *Wie*
human being: *Menschsein, Mensch*

immediate: *unmittelbar, nächste*
in advance: *im vorhinein*
incalculability: *Unberechenbarkeit*
indefinite (and vague): *unbestimmt*
indicate: *anzeigen*
indication (formal): *(formale) Anzeige*
indicative: *anzeigend*
industry (industriousness): *Betrieb*
in each case: *je, jeweils, jeweilig*
inexplicit: *unausdrücklich, unabgehoben*
initially: *zunächst*
in-order-to (the): *Wozu*
interpret (with respect to, on the
basis of, and with a view to): *auslegen (auf)*
interpretation: *Auslegung*
interrogate (with respect to, on the
basis of, and with a view to):
befragen (auf)
investigating (which pursues): *Verfolgen, Nachgehen*
involved in (to be): *dabeisein*
involved in (to become): *mitgehen*
issue (to be at i. [and come to]):
ankommen

kairological: *kairologisch*
know one's way around: *sich auskennen*

leap: *Sprung*
leap forward (anticipatory l. f. and
running in advance): *Vorsprung*
linger (hold itself and): *sich halten*
look (in the direction of, toward, at)
(v.): *hinsehen (auf)*
looking (in the direction of, toward,
at): *Blick, Hinsehen (auf)*
looking-into: *Zusehen*
look into: *zusehen*

make known (announce and):
kundgeben
man: *Mensch*
manner: *Weise*
mask (masking, masquerade): *Maske*
mask (to): *maskieren*
mean-ing: *Vermeinen, Meinen*
means to (being a): *dienlich*
mode: *Weise*
moment (how matters look in the):
Augenblick
motion: *Bewegung*

motivate: *motivieren*
motive: *Motiv*
movement: *Bewegtheit*

no-one (the): *Niemand*
now: *jetzig, jetzt*

observe: *betrachten*
one: *man*
one-self (pron., n.): *man selbst*
on the basis of (from out of and): *aus*
on the basis of (with respect to, o. t.
     b. o., and with a view to): *auf,
     daraufhin, daraufzu*
on the basis of which (wherefrom,
     out of which, and): *woraus*
on-the-basis-of-which (the where-
     from, out-of-which, and): *Woraus*
on-the-basis-of-which (the with-re-
     spect-to-which and): *Woraufhin*
ontic: *ontisch*
ontological: *ontologisch*
open up: *öffnen*
oppressiveness: *Aufdringlichkeit*
origin: *Ursprung*
original: *ursprünglich*
out for and going toward (to be): *aus-
     sein auf*
out of (from): *aus*
out of which (wherefrom, o. o. w.,
     and on the basis of which): *woraus*
out-of-which (the): *Woraus*
out-of-which (the wherefrom, o.,
     and on-the-basis-of-which):
     Woraus
own (our): *eigen, Eigenheit*

particular (temporally): *jeweilig*
particular time (in each case for a
     while at the): *jeweilig, jeweils,
     jeweilen*
path: *Weg*
path (anticipatory apprehension
     which prepares a p. in advance):
     Vorwegnahme
path (anticipatory forehaving which
     prepares a p. in advance):
     Vorweghaben
path of looking (toward): *Blickbahn
     (auf)*
perceptual: *vernehmend*
place (to): *stellen*
point and signify: *be-deuten*

point of departure: *Ausgang*
point of view: *Hinsicht*
point of view which looks in the di-
     rection of and at: *Hinblick auf*
position (n.): *Stand, Stellung*
position of (for) looking (position
     which looks at): *Blickstand,
     Blickstellung*
precautionary measure: *Vorkehrung*
prediction and advance calculation:
     Vorausberechnung
presence: *Präsenz*
present (made): *gegenwärtig, präsent*
present (make): *präsentieren,
     repräsentieren, vergegenwärtigen*
present (the): *Gegenwart*
presenting (presentation):
     Vergegenwärtigung, Vorstellung
preservation (ability of p. to hold
     onto the past): *Behaltbarkeit*
preserve: *behalten, erhalten*
press forth: *drängen, aufdrängen,
     hereindrängen*
primordial: *ursprünglich*
primordiality: *Ursprünglichkeit*
produce: *herstellen*
producing: *Herstellen*
proper: *eigentlich*
public (in the public realm): *öffentlich*
publicness (open space of):
     Öffentlichkeit
public realm: *Öffentlichkeit*
pull (the): *Zug*
pursue: *betreiben, nachgehen, verfolgen*
pursuing: *Verfolgen, Nachgehen*
pursuits: *Betreiben*
put forth initially and bring into
     play: *einsetzen*
put forward: *präsentieren, repräsentieren*
put into place: *stellen*
putting into place: *Herstellen*

questionable: *fraglich*
questionableness: *Fraglichkeit*

reactivate: *nachvollziehen*
ready-to-hand: *zuhanden*
record (grasp and): *erfassen*
reference: *Verweis, Verweisung*
references (context of): *Ver-
     weisungszusammenhang*
relation (to): *Bezug (auf),
     Zusammenhang*

relief (bring into): *abheben, erheben, herausheben*
representation: *Vorstellung*
respective(ly): *jeweilig, jeweils*
round-about (the): *Um, Umhaftes*
running in advance (adj.): *vorweglaufend*
running in advance (n.): *Vorsprung*
run in advance (something preliminary which r. i. a.): *etwas Vorläufiges*

security (certainty and): *Sicherheit*
seeing: *Sehen, Hinsehen*
seeing-in-such-and-such-a-manner: *So-Sehen*
self-communication and self-understanding: *Selbstverständigung*
self-encounter: *Selbstbegegnung*
self-evidence: *Selbstverständlichkeit*
self-interpretation: *Selbstauslegung*
self-presentation: *Selbstpräsentation*
self-veiling: *Sich-verschleiern*
self-world: *Selbstwelt*
significance: *Bedeutsamkeit*
significant: *bedeutsam*
signify: *bedeuten*
signify and point: *be-deuten*
sojourn (hold itself and): *sich aufhalten*
sojourn (n.): *Aufenthalt*
sojourn (never halting, making a s., and holding out there): *aufenthaltslos*
sojourning (at home in): *Aufhalten (bei)*
soon: *demnächst*
spatiality: *Räumlichkeit*
stance held to: *Haltung*
standpoint: *Standpunkt*
standpoints (freedom from): *Standpunktfreiheit*
starting point: *Ansatz*
stir (grasp and): *ergreifen*
strange (something): *Fremdes*
style: *Stil*
subject matter: *Sache*
suchness: *So*

take up: *ergreifen*
talk (n.): *Gerede*
tarrying for a while (awhile) (at home in, among): *Verweilen (bei), Je-Verweilen*

tarrying-for-a-while (tarrying-awhile): *Verweilen*
temporality: *Zeitlichkeit*
temporalize (and unfold): *zeitigen*
temporalizing (temporalization): *Zeitigung*
temporally particular: *jeweilig*
temporal particularity (awhileness of): *Jeweiligkeit*
tendency: *Tendenz*
tendency of looking toward: *Blicktendenz auf*
there (adv.): *da*
there (character of the): *Da-Charakter*
there (the): *Da*
there (to be): *dasein*
there-for-this (the): *Dafür*
there-in-order-to-do-this (the): *Dazu*
thing (itself): *Sache (selbst), Ding*
those-who-are-there: *Daseiendes*
those-who-are-there-with-us: *Mitdaseiende*
those with us in life: *Mitlebende*
time (a): *(eine) Zeit*
time (at the particular): *jeweilig, jeweils, jeweilen*
to-be-"in"-the-world: *in-der-Welt-sein*
today (adv.) (today's): *heutig, heute*
today (the): *Heute*
toward: *auf*
toward-which (the): *Worauf*
transport (to): *versetzen*
true safeguarding: *Bewahren*
true safekeeping (bring into): *verwahren*
true to life (being): *Lebensnähe*

unconcealed: *unverborgen*
uncover: *aufdecken, entdecken*
uncoveredness: *Entdecktheit*
understand: *verstehen*
understanding: *Verstehen*
unfold (temporalize and): *zeitigen*
unpredictability: *Unberechenbarkeit*

vague (indefinite and): *unbestimmt*
view: *Blick*

wakeful: *wach*
wakefulness: *Wachsein*
way (of pointing): *Weise*
what (the): *Was*
wherefrom, out of which, and on the basis of which: *woraus*

wherefrom, out-of-which, and on-the-basis-of-which (the): *Woraus*

wherein: *worin, worum*

wherein (the): *Worin*

whereinto (the): *Wohinein*

whereto (the): *Worauf*

while (n.): *Weile*

while (for a, all the): *jeweilig, jeweils, jeweilen*

while (tarrying for a w. [at home in]): *Verweilen (bei)*

whiling (at home in): *Verweilen (bei), Je-Verweilen*

wide-awake: *wach*

with a view to: *im Absehen auf, Absicht auf, absichtlich*

with a view to (with respect to, on the basis of, and): *auf, daraufhin, daraufzu*

with respect to, on the basis of, and with a view to: *auf, daraufhin, daraufzu*

with-respect-to-which and on-the-basis-of-which (the): *Woraufhin*

with-which (the): *Womit*

with-world: *Mitwelt*

with-world (in the, of the): *mit-weltlich*

working out: *Ausbildung*

work out: *ausbilden*

work out in advance (calculate and): *ausrechnen im vorhinein*

world: *Welt*

worldly: *weltlich*

world round-about: *Umwelt*

worried: *bekümmert*

worry (n.): *Bekümmerung*